United States Government Accountability Office

Report to the Chairman, Committee on Commerce, Science and Transportation, U.S. Senate

August 2013

INTERSTATE COMPACTS

I0448366

Transparency and Oversight of Bi-State Tolling Authorities Could Be Enhanced

GAO Highlights

Highlights of GAO-13-687, a report to the Chairman, Committee on Commerce, Science and Transportation, U.S. Senate

INTERSTATE COMPACTS

Transparency and Oversight of Bi-State Tolling Authorities Could Be Enhanced

Why GAO Did This Study

The Northeast is home to some of the most highly traveled interstate crossings in the United States, funded by toll revenues collected from the traveling public. Since 1921, Congress has provided its consent to New York, New Jersey, Pennsylvania, and Delaware to enter into legal agreements known as interstate compacts, establishing four bi-state tolling authorities to build and maintain toll bridges and tunnels. In recent years, bi-state tolling authorities have come under scrutiny for toll increases and other concerns, and GAO was asked to review their toll-setting decisions and oversight framework. GAO examined: (1) the authority of bi-state tolling authorities to set and use tolls and the factors that influence toll setting; (2) the extent to which the authorities involve and inform the public in toll-setting decisions; and (3) the extent to which the authorities are subject to external and internal oversight. GAO reviewed federal and state laws, bi-state tolling authority documents, and interviewed officials from the authorities and state audit offices. GAO does not make recommendations to non-federal entities; nonetheless the authorities could benefit from greater transparency in public involvement and clearer lines of external oversight. DOT had no comments on a draft of this report and three authorities provided technical comments, which GAO incorporated as appropriate. In addition, the Port Authority of New York and New Jersey disagreed, stating its policies constituted a documented public involvement process. GAO maintains that these policies were not publicly available, or a defined and structured process.

View GAO-13-687. For more information, contact Susan Fleming at (202) 512-2834 or flemings@gao.gov.

What GAO Found

Bi-state tolling authorities have broad authority to set toll rates and use revenues for a range of purposes, including maintaining, repairing, and improving their infrastructure. In setting tolls, bi-state tolling authorities are primarily influenced by debt obligations and maintain specific operating revenues to repay their debt. A federal statute requiring bridge tolls to be "just and reasonable" has less influence on tolling decisions, in part, because no federal agency has authority to enforce the standard.

Bi-state tolling authorities are not required to follow federal or general state requirements for involving and informing the public; they set their own policies that can be less stringent than practices of transportation agencies that follow federal or state requirements. In their most recent toll increases, the bi-state authorities generally provided the public limited opportunities to learn about and comment on proposed toll rates before they were approved. For example, one bi-state authority did not hold any public toll hearings, while another provided one day for hearings. In contrast to federal and general state requirements and leading practices, the bi-state authorities did not in all cases (1) have documented public involvement procedures for toll setting; (2) provide the public with key information on the toll proposals in advance of public hearings; (3) offer the public sufficient opportunities to comment on toll proposals; and (4) provide a public summary of comments received before toll increases were approved.

External oversight of the bi-state authorities is limited as only one of the four authorities has been regularly audited by a state audit entity. While these audits have uncovered areas of concern, the authority of most state audit entities to oversee the bi-state authorities is unclear. Differences in states' laws and disagreements between the bi-state authorities and state audit agencies have raised questions about the authority of several states to provide oversight. Each of the four bi-state authorities provides some internal oversight, but one has not established access authority for its inspector general, which, as a result, lacks an assurance of independence. Because internal auditors are generally not required under internal audit standards to report to outside audiences, the public may lack knowledge of their efforts to ensure accountability for the use of toll revenues.

Interstate Bridges and Tunnels Owned by Bi-State Tolling Authorities

Bi-State authority	Tolled interstate bridges and tunnels
Delaware River and Bay Authority	1 toll bridge: Delaware Memorial Bridge
Delaware River Joint Toll Bridge Commission	7 toll bridges, including the I-78, Milford-Montague, Delaware Water Gap, and Portland-Columbia Bridges
Delaware River Port Authority	4 toll bridges, including the Ben Franklin, Betsy Ross, Walt Whitman, and Commodore Barry Bridges
Port Authority of New York and New Jersey	4 toll bridges, 2 toll tunnels, including the George Washington, Bayonne, and Goethals Bridges; Holland, and Lincoln Tunnels

Source: GAO analysis of bi-state tolling authority documents.

Contents

Figure

Abbreviations

DRBA	Delaware River and Bay Authority
DRJTBC	Delaware River Joint Toll Bridge Commission
DRPA	Delaware River Port Authority
DOT	Department of Transportation
FHWA	Federal Highway Administration
FTA	Federal Transit Administration
MPO	metropolitan planning organization
NJDOT	New Jersey Department of Transportation
PANYNJ	Port Authority of New York and New Jersey
PATCO	Port Authority Transit Corporation
PATH	Port Authority Trans-Hudson

GAO

U.S. GOVERNMENT ACCOUNTABILITY OFFICE

441 G St. N.W.
Washington, DC 20548

August 15, 2013

The Honorable John D. Rockefeller IV
Chairman
Committee on Commerce, Science and Transportation
United States Senate

Dear Mr. Chairman:

The Northeast is home to some of the most highly-traveled interstate crossings in the United States, including the George Washington and Delaware Memorial Bridges, which are funded by toll revenues collected from the traveling public. These toll bridges, along with more than a dozen others as well as several tunnels, are owned and maintained by several entities, which we refer to as bi-state tolling authorities. These authorities are created through legal agreements, known as interstate compacts, between two or more states to act cooperatively to address matters of interest to both states, such as operating ports and interstate toll crossings. Congress must give its consent to states to enter into interstate compacts that affect the balance of power between the federal government and the states or affect a power constitutionally assigned to the federal government, such as the power to regulate interstate commerce. With Congress' consent, Delaware, New Jersey, New York, and Pennsylvania have entered into interstate compacts and created four bi-state tolling authorities to build, maintain, and operate certain interstate crossings.

Since 1921, Congress has granted its consent to a total of seven interstate compacts to manage toll bridges or tunnels crossing state boundaries; four of those compacts are currently administered by bi-state state tolling authorities: the Delaware River and Bay Authority (DRBA), the Delaware River Joint Toll Bridge Commission (DRJTBC), the Delaware River Port Authority (DRPA), and the Port Authority of New

York and New Jersey (PANYNJ).[1] These bi-state tolling authorities are primarily funded through toll collections or from revenues generated by other activities—such as fees and rents from airports, maritime ports, or other assets they may own and manage—and generally do not receive state funds. For example, the DRBA owns and manages the Delaware Memorial Bridge connecting New Jersey and Delaware, five regional airports, two ferry lines operating on the Delaware Bay and River, and other facilities. As we have reported, these authorities operate with congressional consent but are neither federal in nature nor state in scope; they occupy what some have referred to as a "third tier" of government.[2]

The federal role in reviewing bridge toll rates set by bi-state tolling authorities is limited in scope and has diminished over time. Since 1906, federal law has required that toll rates for bridges over navigable waters be "just and reasonable."[3] The Department of Transportation's (DOT) Federal Highway Administration (FHWA) previously enforced the requirement by conducting administrative reviews of toll rates if complaints were made by third parties or under the FHWA Administrator's discretion. In 1987, Congress repealed DOT's review authority; however, the just and reasonable standard remains in law.[4] In 2011, legislation was introduced but not enacted to reinstate DOT's authority to review toll

---

[1]In addition to DRBA, DRJTBC, DRPA, and PANYNJ, the three other congressionally consented interstate compacts are the (1) New Jersey-Pennsylvania Turnpike Bridge Compact, (2) Missouri River Toll Bridge Compact, and the (3) Portsmouth-Kittery Bridge Compact. These three were not included in our review because their facilities are either not currently in operation (as is the case in the Missouri River Toll Bridge Compact) or the facilities are not managed by bi-state tolling authorities, but rather by the departments of transportation for the respective states entering into the compacts.

[2]See GAO, *Interstate Compacts: An Overview of the Structure and Governance of Environment and Natural Resource Compacts*, GAO-07-519 (Washington, D.C.: Apr. 3, 2007).

[3]The current requirement that tolls on bridges be just and reasonable is found at 33 U.S.C. § 508. Appendix II discusses the evolution of the "just and reasonable" standard and how it has been applied.

[4]Surface Transportation Uniform Relocation and Assistance Act of 1987; Pub. L. No. 100-17, § 135, 101 Stat. 132, 173 (1987).

rates, either upon complaint or under the initiative of the Secretary of Transportation.[5] To date, such legislation has not been reintroduced.

Federal oversight of the bi-state tolling authorities is generally limited to those programs receiving federal funding and does not include the management of the interstate toll crossings. The Federal Transit Administration (FTA) or Federal Aviation Administration may provide funding to transit systems or airports that are operated by bi-state tolling authorities, and oversee those funds to ensure they are spent according to federal requirements. To help redevelop the lower Manhattan area after 9/11, for instance, the FTA allocated $2.9 billion to the PANYNJ to construct a transportation hub at the World Trade Center. In October 2012, the construction site for the World Trade Center transportation hub and portions of the Port Authority Trans-Hudson (PATH) commuter rail line were flooded and certain PANYNJ facilities were severely damaged by Hurricane Sandy. In response, FTA has allocated $1.36 billion to the PANYNJ for emergency repairs, restoration, and to increase the resiliency of the PATH system to guard against future disasters.[6]

In recent years, certain bi-state tolling authorities have come under public scrutiny regarding toll increases and concerns that revenues have been used for purposes beyond maintaining critical transportation infrastructure. In addition, recent management audits by outside consultants and state audit agencies have raised concerns about the extent to which these authorities are accountable and transparent to the public. You asked us to review the toll-setting and oversight framework of the bi-state tolling authorities. We examined: (1) the authority of bi-state tolling authorities to set and use tolls and the factors that influence toll

---

[5]Commuter Protection Act, S. 2006 and H.R. 3684 112th Cong. (2011). This legislation would have reinstated DOT's authority to review toll rates for any bridge or tunnel constructed under the authority of several federal bridge acts—the Bridge Act of 1906 (33 U.S.C. § 491 et seq.), the General Bridge Act of 1946 (33 U.S.C. § 525 et seq.) or the International Bridge Act of 1972 (33 U.S.C. § 535 et seq.)—and over or through any bridge or tunnel constructed on a federal-aid highway (as defined in 23 U.S.C. § 101(a)).

[6]The Disaster Relief Appropriations Act, 2013 (Pub. L. No. 113-2, div. A, 127 Stat. 4, 35 (2013)) provided $10.9 billion to FTA's Emergency Relief Program for recovery, relief, and resiliency efforts in areas affected by Hurricane Sandy. However, as a result of the Budget Control Act of 2011 (Pub. L. No. 112-25), 5 percent of the $10.9 billion made available under the Appropriations Act ($545,000,000) is subject to the significant spending cuts known as sequestration and is unavailable for Hurricane Sandy Disaster Relief. See 78 Fed. Reg. 19357 (Mar. 29, 2013). As of May 29, 2013, FTA had allocated about $5.7 billion for transit relief in New York and New Jersey.

setting; (2) the extent to which bi-state tolling authorities involve and inform the public in their toll-setting decisions; and (3) the extent to which the bi-state tolling authorities are subject to external and internal oversight.

To examine these issues, we gathered information from the four bi-state tolling authorities currently operating tolled interstate crossings under an interstate compact: the DRBA, DRJTBC, DRPA, and PANYNJ. To identify the factors considered in setting toll rates, we interviewed officials from each of these authorities and reviewed financial statements and related documents describing the factors contributing to their toll rates. To assess the purposes for which toll revenues can be used, we reviewed the interstate compacts, bylaws, and other documentation. While we reviewed the allowable uses for toll revenues, due to ongoing litigation between the PANYNJ and the American Automobile Association regarding recent toll increases by the PANYNJ, we did not assess the specific purposes and projects for which the PANYNJ uses its toll revenues. For consistency, we did not assess the specific purposes and projects for which the other bi-state tolling authorities use their toll revenue. To assess the extent to which the bi-state tolling authorities involve and inform the public in their toll-setting decisions, we reviewed documentation on their most recent toll increases as provided by each of the bi-state tolling authorities and collected from their public web sites. We compared their public involvement practices to those of federal, state, and local transportation authorities, including tolling authorities in Michigan and California that were not created by interstate compacts. To assess the external and internal oversight of the bi-state authorities, we reviewed available audit reports and interviewed and collected information from the state audit agencies of each of the four states in our review (Delaware, New Jersey, New York, and Pennsylvania) and from the internal audit organizations within the bi-state authorities. We compared the external oversight structure with GAO's *Government Auditing Standards* and other relevant auditing standards and other GAO work on oversight of non-federal entities.[7] We compared the activities of

---

[7]GAO, *Government Auditing Standards: 2011 Revision*, GAO-12-331G (Washington, D.C.: December 2011); International Organization of Supreme Audit Institutions, *General Standards in Government Auditing and Standards with Ethical Significance*, ISSAI 200 (Vienna, Austria: 2001); GAO, *Inspectors General: Proposals to Strengthen Independence and Accountability*, GAO-07-1021T (Washington, D.C.: June 20, 2007); and GAO, *United Nations: Status of Internal Oversight Services*, GAO/NSIAD-98-9 (Washington, D.C.: Nov. 19, 1997).

the internal audit entities with the *International Standards for the Professional Practice of Internal Auditing* published by the Institute of Internal Auditors and related GAO work on internal auditing.[8]

We conducted this performance audit from July 2012 through August 2013 in accordance with generally accepted government auditing standards. Those standards require that we plan and perform the audit to obtain sufficient, appropriate evidence to provide a reasonable basis for our findings and conclusions based on our audit objectives. We believe that the evidence obtained provides a reasonable basis for our findings and conclusions based on our audit objectives. Our objectives, scope, and methodology are discussed in more detail in appendix I.

Background

Interstate compacts are legal agreements between states designed to address issues that transcend state lines. Compacts enable states to act jointly on matters that are beyond the authority of an individual state but are not within the specific purview of the federal government. States have entered into interstate compacts to act jointly to address a variety of concerns including resolving border disputes, allocating interstate waters, enhancing law enforcement, disposing of radioactive waste, and developing regional transportation systems, among other issues.[9] According to the Council of State Governments, more than 200 interstate compacts exist today, and most of those are for purposes other than managing interstate crossings. To form an interstate compact, two or more states typically negotiate an agreement, and each state legislature enacts a law that is identical to the agreement reached. Once all states specified in the compact have enacted such laws, the compact is formed.[10]

In cases where the compact affects the balance of power between the federal government and the states, the states must obtain the consent of Congress for the compact to be valid. Congress can give its consent by passing legislation that specifically recognizes the compact as enacted by

---

[8]The Institute of Internal Auditors, *Professional Practices Framework, International Standards for the Professional Practice of Internal Auditing,* (Altamonte Springs, FL: Oct. 2012); GAO/NSIAD-98-9; GAO-07-1021T.

[9]GAO-07-519.

[10]GAO-07-519.

the states, at which time the compact becomes federal law.[11] Congress may impose conditions as part of granting its consent, and it typically reserves the right to alter, amend, or repeal its consent in the compact itself. Congress included such a provision in each of the public laws consenting to the four interstate compacts in this review.

In establishing an interstate compact, states usually delegate authority to an independent entity, such as a bi-state tolling authority, that is created to administer and implement the compact's provisions. Decision-making for each bi-state tolling authority is the responsibility of a board of commissioners composed of representatives of the member states, who are appointed by a state's governor, such as local government officials, or serve by virtue of their elected position, such as a state treasurer. In addition to appointing commissioners, state governors may have authority to veto decisions made by commissioners from their state if such authority is specified in the compact or provided through reciprocal legislation passed by the states. The interstate compact includes the terms to which both states have agreed, and to which Congress has provided its consent. Some compacts include language that enables states to modify a compact through reciprocal legislation.[12] Unless the bi-state authorities engage in programs that receive federal funds, such as operating transit systems or airports, they are generally not subject to federal oversight.[13]

---

[11]Congress may also recognize an interstate compact in advance by passing legislation encouraging states to enter into a specified compact or compacts for specified purposes, or by implication after the fact, when actions by the states and the federal government indicate that Congress has granted its consent even in the absence of a specific legislative act. GAO-07-519.

[12]The DRPA, PANYNJ, and DRBA compacts include this type of language, while the DRJTBC compact does not. See *Int'l Union of Operating Eng'rs, Local 542 v. Del. River Joint Toll Bridge Comm.*, 311 F3d 273 (3d Cir. 2002) for a discussion of how various courts have interpreted this type of language.

[13]The DRJTBC's 1992 agreement with the U.S. Department of Transportation, the New Jersey Department of Transportation, and the Pennsylvania Department of Transportation under 23 U.S.C. § 129 permits the use of federal-aid highway funding to pay for the construction and upkeep of the I-78 Toll Bridge and requires that all toll revenues are used for debt service, reasonable return on private investment, and operation and maintenance. The Moving Ahead for Progress in the 21st Century Act (MAP-21) imposes a new requirement for annual audits to ensure compliance with these limitations, the results of which must be transmitted to the Department of Transportation. Pub. L. No. 112-141, § 1512, 126 Stat. 405, 567 (2012).

The four bi-state tolling authorities manage a wide range of facilities, but the PANYNJ is significantly larger than the other three in terms of assets owned. At the end of fiscal year 2011, the PANYNJ reported that the total value of its assets was approximately $33.9 billion, which includes its five airports, six tolled crossings between New York and New Jersey, the World Trade Center properties, and other assets. By comparison, the DRPA's $1.8 billion in total assets in 2011 was the next-largest asset value. New Jersey has a unique stake in these bi-state tolling authorities as it is the only state that is a party to each of the four interstate compacts in our review. See table 1 for a summary of the assets maintained by the four bi-state tolling authorities in our review.

Table 1: Facilities Managed by the Four Bi-State Tolling Authorities with Interstate Compacts

Bi-state tolling authority and location	Compact states and year of congressional consent	Transportation facilities and other properties	Total asset value, fiscal year 2011 (dollars in billions)
Port Authority of New York and New Jersey (PANYNJ) New York City Metropolitan Area	New Jersey and New York 1921	• 4 toll bridges and 2 toll tunnels: George Washington, Bayonne, and Goethals Bridges and the Outerbridge Crossing; Holland and Lincoln Tunnels • 188 non-toll highway bridges: 109 bridges in New York and 79 bridges in New Jersey • 5 airports: John F. Kennedy International, LaGuardia, Newark Liberty International, Stewart International, and Teterboro Airports • 7 port terminals: Brooklyn-Port Authority, Elizabeth-Port Authority, Greenville Yard-Port Authority, Howland Hook, and Port Jersey-Port Authority Marine Terminals; Port Newark and Red Hook Container Terminal • Transit and ferry assets: Port Authority Trans-Hudson (PATH) Rail Transit System, Journal Square Transportation Center, Port Authority Bus Terminal, George Washington Bridge Bus Station, World Trade Center Transportation Hub, New York Harbor Commuter Ferry system • Other properties: World Trade Center, Waterfront Development in Queens and Hoboken, and several industrial parks and real estate developments in the New York metropolitan area	$33.9
Delaware River Port Authority (DRPA) Philadelphia, PA & Camden, NJ	New Jersey and Pennsylvania 1931	• 4 toll bridges: Ben Franklin, Betsy Ross, Walt Whitman, and Commodore Barry Bridges • Transit system and ferry assets: Port Authority Transit Corporation (PATCO), RiverLink Ferry • Other properties: Various real estate investments in the Delaware River Port District	$1.836

Bi-state tolling authority and location	Compact states and year of congressional consent	Transportation facilities and other properties	Total asset value, fiscal year 2011 (dollars in billions)
Delaware River Joint Toll Bridge Commission (DRJTBC) Border of Philadelphia and Bucks Counties, PA to NJ/NY state line	New Jersey and Pennsylvania 1935	• 7 toll bridges: I-78, Milford-Montague, Delaware Water Gap, Portland-Columbia, Easton-Phillipsburg, New Hope-Lambertville, Morrisville-Trenton Toll Bridges • 13 non-toll bridges supported by revenues from 7 toll bridges	$0.815
Delaware River and Bay Authority (DRBA) Delaware and the counties of Gloucester, Salem, Cumberland, and Cape May, New Jersey	New Jersey and Delaware 1962	• 1 toll bridge: Delaware Memorial Bridge • 5 airports: New Castle Airport, Cape May Airport, Millville Airport, Civil Air Terminal at Dover AFB, Delaware Airpark • 2 ferries: Cape May-Lewes Ferry, Three Forts Ferry Crossing • Other properties: Salem County Business Park, located in Carney's Point Township, New Jersey; Riverfront Marketplace, Wilmington, Delaware	$0.632

Source: GAO analysis of bi-state tolling authority documents.

NOTE: Total asset value represents the value of transportation facilities and properties as well as other assets.

The bi-state tolling authorities primarily fund the operation and maintenance of these facilities through tolls and other user fees collected from assets they manage. Many of these bridges and tunnels require significant renovations due to their age, and the costs of maintaining these facilities are substantial. For example, the PANYNJ began construction on the George Washington Bridge in 1927 and the bridge opened to traffic in 1931. Approximately 270,000 vehicles cross it every day, and the PANYNJ plans to spend $544 million to replace the suspender ropes on the bridge from 2011 through 2020. Each of the bi-state tolling authorities has instituted a toll increase in the past 5 years to help fund such renovations, and the toll rates may vary based on the type of vehicle crossing the facility (e.g., passenger vehicles or commercial trucks), whether cash or electronic payment (EZPass) is used, and the time of day. For example, the PANYNJ, which collects tolls from eastbound drivers entering New York City on its facilities, raised the toll rates for automobiles paying cash from $8 to $12 in September 2011, with an additional increase of $1 for cash tolls in December 2012 and additional $1 increases effective in December 2014 and December 2015. Passenger vehicles using EZPass pay less—$8.25 during off-peak hours and $10.25 during peak hours. See table 2 for an overview of the passenger vehicle toll rate ranges and bi-state tolling authorities' operating revenues and expenses in fiscal year 2011.

Table 2: Bi-State Tolling Authorities' Current Passenger-Vehicle Cash Toll Rates and 2011 Operating Revenues

Bi-state tolling authority	Passenger vehicle toll rate range as of July 2013[a]	Toll bridge and tunnel operating revenues, 2011 (Dollars in millions)	Other operating revenues, 2011 (Dollars in millions)	Total operating revenues, 2011 (Dollars in millions)
PANYNJ	$8.25 to $13.00[b]	$1,079[c]	$2,721	$3,800
DRPA	$5.00	$268	$32	$300
DRBA	$4.00[d]	$86	$29	$115
DRJTBC	$.60 to $1.00[e]	$103	$1	$104

Source: GAO analysis of bi-state tolling authority data and annual reports, 2011.

[a]Each of the four bi-state tolling authorities collects tolls one-way.

[b]The PANYNJ charges an EZPass rate of $10.25 during peak hours (weekdays between 6 and 10 AM and between 4 and 8 PM; weekends between 11 AM and 9 PM) and $8.25 for all other (off-peak) hours on all 6 crossings. The PANYNJ also offers discounted rate plans for its six crossings for eligible carpools ($4.25) and certain low-emission vehicles ($4.75); and reduced rates for certain vehicles crossing the Goethals Bridge, Outerbridge Crossing or Bayonne Bridge from Staten Island ($5.25).

[c]PANYNJ operating revenues also include the Port Authority Bus Terminal and the George Washington Bridge Bus Station.

[d]The DRBA offers a commuter plan for $25 that allows 25 trips across the Delaware Memorial Bridge valid for 30 days.

[e]The DRJTBC offers an EZPass discounted price of $.60 per trip if the vehicle makes 20 or more trips in 35 days.

To secure financing for capital improvements to their facilities, bi-state tolling authorities issue bonds to creditors and pledge tolls and other revenues for the repayment of the bond principal and interest. The four bi-state tolling authorities are required through either their bond agreements with creditors or bylaws to have an annual audit of their consolidated financial statements by an independent audit firm, which provides assurance that financial information reported to the public is accurate and fairly presented. These audits are generally not designed to evaluate the effectiveness of an entity's internal controls or management's overall performance in achieving its objectives, but are meant to provide assurance that the financial information provided to creditors and the public—including assets, liabilities, revenues, and expenditures—are free from material misstatement.

In recent years, the operations of two bi-state tolling authorities, the DRPA and the PANYNJ, have been the subject of public scrutiny and media attention. In response, the governors of New York, New Jersey, and Pennsylvania directed the authorities to allow reviews that identified concerns about the management and operations of the two authorities. Specifically, as a condition of the governors' approval of the PANYNJ's 2011 toll increase, the PANYNJ contracted with two consulting firms to undertake a comprehensive review and audit of the PANYNJ's finances and operations. Generally, this audit (1) found, among other things, concerns with the PANYNJ capital-planning process, cost controls, and oversight of the World Trade Center program, and (2) summarized reform initiatives undertaken by PANYNJ to address concerns.[14] In July 2010, the governors of New Jersey and Pennsylvania directed the DRPA to agree to an independent investigation of its operations by the New Jersey Office of the State Comptroller. The State Comptroller found issues with the transparency of DRPA's practice of sharing insurance commissions, providing unlimited free bridge passes to DRPA employees, and the conduct of its economic development program.[15] DRPA has passed several board resolutions to address concerns. During the course of our review, DRPA reported that its economic development program was under review by a federal grand jury led by the U.S. Attorney's Office in Philadelphia.

Bi-State Tolling Authorities Have Broad Authority to Set and Use Tolls, and Tolling Decisions Are Primarily Influenced by Debt Rather Than Federal Toll Provisions

Interstate compacts provide the bi-state tolling authorities with broad authority to set toll rates and use revenues for a range of purposes, including capital improvements for their transportation infrastructure and, in certain cases, economic development projects. In setting tolls, bi-state tolling authorities are primarily influenced by bond agreements, as well as operations and maintenance costs and other factors. To obtain financing for capital projects, bi-state authorities pledge through bond agreements to maintain specific revenue required to repay their debt. The bi-state authorities set toll rates to meet these revenue requirements, while also accounting for the costs of maintaining the infrastructure given economic conditions, traffic levels, and other factors. Federal law has less influence on tolling decisions because currently no federal agency has the authority to enforce the federal requirement that bridge tolls be "just and reasonable." In addition, some federal courts have questioned whether a private party has the right to challenge toll increases in court under this requirement. However, private parties also have been able to challenge

---

[14]Navigant, *Phase I Interim Report: Presented to the Special Committee of the Board of Commissioners, PANYNJ* (Jan. 31, 2012). Also see Navigant, *Phase II Report: Presented to the Special Committee of the Board of Commissioners, PANYNJ* (Sept. 2012); also see Rothschild, *Final Report: Presented to the Special Committee of the Board of Commissioners, PANYNJ* (Sept. 2012).

[15]New Jersey Office of the State Comptroller, *Investigative Report: Delaware River Port Authority* (Trenton, NJ: Mar. 29, 2012).

toll increases in federal court under the Commerce Clause of the U.S. Constitution.[16]

Bi-State Tolling Authorities Have Broad Authority to Set Toll Rates and Use Toll Revenues

The interstate compacts generally provide the bi-state tolling authorities with broad authority to set rates and use toll revenues to maintain, repair, and improve their transportation infrastructure and cover other expenses. Although the specific language in the interstate compacts varies, the bi-state authorities are permitted to set tolls and use tolls and other revenues for bridges, tunnels, and other infrastructure. The bi-state authorities are also generally permitted to use tolls and other revenues to cover operations and maintenance costs, make capital improvements, repay debt obligations, maintain reserve funds to address contingencies, or to make other investments. The bi-state tolling authorities prepare capital plans that prioritize their large-scale projects to improve and maintain their facilities, such as bridge resurfacing, painting and de-leading, and replacing and repairing bridge cables and transit cars over a period of several years. For example, PANYNJ officials reported that over the past 5 years, the PANYNJ has spent approximately $2.5 billion on capital projects for its "interstate transportation network," which includes its bridge, tunnel, PATH train system, and bus and ferry facilities. Similarly, DRPA's approved 2013 capital plan identifies more than $746 million in capital improvement projects for its four bridges, transit line, and other facilities over the next 5 years. The DRPA reported that in 2010, its board approved two contracts totaling nearly $140 million to replace the deck of the Walt Whitman Bridge and monitor construction of the project. Bi-state authorities are also permitted to use toll revenues to subsidize other operations, such as transit services. For example, the DRPA reported that in its 2012 capital plan, it provided about $33 million to its PATCO train line for capital projects, such as rehabilitating tracks and other improvements, representing about 26 percent of its total capital program for that year.

In addition to using tolls and other revenues for transportation purposes, the PANYNJ, the DRPA, and the DRBA are permitted by either their compact, subsequent compact amendments or bi-state legislation to use revenues for projects to promote their local economies, such as airports,

---

[16]The Commerce Clause provides Congress with the power to "regulate Commerce... among the several states..." U.S. Const. art. 1, § 8, cl. 3.

industrial parks, business centers, and waterfront development projects.[17] In certain cases the compacts impose conditions on using revenue for economic development. For example, the DRPA is permitted to use revenues for economic development only after allocating revenues to fund operations and maintenance costs for bridge and other capital facilities.[18] According to DRJTBC officials, its compact does not authorize the DRJTBC to use its toll revenues for economic development projects.

Tolling Decisions Are Primarily Driven by Debt Obligations and Other Factors

The bi-state authorities set tolls and other charges primarily to generate revenues to maintain their operations and infrastructure and meet their debt obligations. On a year-to-year basis, the bi-state tolling authorities' annual revenues may not be sufficient to fund the infrastructure projects in their long-term capital programs. The authorities enter into bond agreements with creditors in which they pledge the collection of tolls, among other revenues, to secure financing for capital improvements. Such bond agreements provide the authorities with the funding they need to maintain their infrastructure in a state of good repair, but this also can result in the bi-state tolling authorities incurring substantial debt obligations, which must be repaid over time. For example, the four bi-state authorities' total debt service costs, including the principal and cost of interest, range from $453 million to $30.2 billion over the life of their bonds, which may extend several decades depending on the bond terms. See table 3 for a summary of the principal owed by the four authorities on their bond debt and the total debt service cost over the life of their bonds.

[17]As previously noted, we reviewed the allowable uses for toll revenues, but due to ongoing litigation between the PANYNJ and the American Automobile Association regarding recent toll increases by the PANYNJ, we did not assess the specific purposes and projects for which the PANYNJ uses its toll revenues. For consistency, we did not assess the specific purposes and projects for which the other bi-state tolling authorities use their toll revenues.

[18]DRPA reported that its board passed a resolution in 2011 that limited its economic development spending to the completion of seven existing projects. This is discussed further later in this report.

Table 3: Bi-State Tolling Authorities' Bond Debt Principal and Total Debt Service Cost, as of December 2011 (Dollars in millions)

	DRBA	DRJTBC	DRPA	PANYNJ
Bond debt principal	$284	$406	$1,333	$15,751
Total debt service cost	$453	$674	$1,861	$30,219

Source: Bi-state tolling authority annual reports, audit reports and/or financial statements, December 2011.

Note: All dollar amounts in table are rounded to the nearest million. The total debt service cost varies based on the life of the bonds.

Bi-state tolling authorities maintain specific operating revenue levels to pay the annual principal and interest on their debt. One measure of an entity's ability to repay its debt is the "debt service coverage ratio," which compares an entity's annual operating revenues after operating expenses (net revenues) to its annual debt service costs. For example, the DRJTBC is required through a bond agreement to maintain a debt service coverage ratio of 1.3—meaning that it must generate net revenues that are at least 130 percent of its annual debt service costs or risk a default on its debt.[19] Officials from each of the four bi-state tolling authorities reported that they monitor revenues on an ongoing basis and adjust their toll rates, in part, to ensure that future revenues will be adequate to meet their debt coverage requirements. Officials from Moody's Investors Service, a credit-rating agency, stated that they use the debt service coverage ratio as a metric to assess the credit-worthiness of entities seeking financing through capital markets. Credit-rating agency officials reported that the ability to set toll rates independently to cover debt obligations is the most important factor considered in assigning a credit rating.

Bi-state tolling authorities also consider in their toll-setting decisions forecasts of traffic and associated toll revenues. These forecasts are based upon projections of economic factors that underlie traffic demand, such as employment, population, value of goods and services, fuel prices, and other factors that can affect traffic volume and associated toll revenues. For example, officials from the PANYNJ reported that more

---

[19]DRJTBC reported that it has adopted a policy in consultation with credit-rating agencies to maintain a debt–service coverage ratio of 1.5, or risk a downgrade of its credit ratings and less favorable terms on future debt.

than 127 million cars, buses, and trucks crossed its bridges and tunnels in 2007. The PANYNJ reported that as a result of the economic recession, elevated gas prices, and its toll increase, traffic declined by about 6 percent to approximately 119 million vehicle crossings in 2011. Additionally, unforeseen weather events that can cause damage to infrastructure can affect revenues and expenses; the bi-state tolling authorities maintain a reserve fund and insure their assets for such events.

A Federal Law That Tolls Be "Just and Reasonable" Has Less Influence on Toll-Setting Decisions Than Other Factors

Although there is a federal statute requiring that bridge tolls be "just and reasonable,"[20] in practice this requirement has less influence on bi-state authorities' toll-setting decisions than other factors, in that no federal agency currently has the authority to enforce the standard. Since 1906, federal law has required that toll rates for bridges over navigable waters be "just and reasonable," and until 1987 this provision was enforced by various federal agencies. Originally, the Department of War performed this role, and later the Department of Transportation's (DOT) Federal Highway Administration (FHWA) performed an administrative review of toll rates if complaints were made by third parties or at the FHWA Administrator's discretion. From 1970 to 1987, the FHWA Administrator adjudicated several significant toll increase challenges, finding on at least two occasions that proposed toll rates were unjust and unreasonable, and on at least one occasion that proposed toll rates met the "just and reasonable" standard. In 1987, Congress repealed DOT's authority to determine if toll rates were just and reasonable,[21] but the standard itself remains in statute. While several parties have sought to challenge toll increases under this federal "just and reasonable" standard in court, certain federal courts have questioned whether private parties have the right to raise such court challenges. However, private parties also have

---

[20]33 U.S.C. § 508.

[21]Surface Transportation and Uniform Relocation Assistance Act of 1987, Pub. L. No. 100-17, § 135, 101 Stat. 132, 173 (Jan. 14, 1987). A Senate report accompanying the act stated in a section-by-section analysis of the act that, "Federal oversight of the reasonableness of tolls has proven to be administratively burdensome [and] legally unproductive." Section-by-Section Analysis of S. 312—Essential Highway Reauthorization Amendments of 1987, 133 Cong. Rec. S778 (Jan. 14, 1987).

been able to challenge toll increases in federal court under the Commerce Clause.[22]

Although no federal agency currently enforces the just and reasonable standard, prior administrative decisions and federal court opinions have interpreted how the standard is to be applied. Since 1973, federal administrative and court decisions have generally found that just and reasonable tolls are those sufficient to pay not only the reasonable cost of maintaining, repairing and operating facilities, but also to establish funds to amortize bridge indebtedness, provide a reasonable return on invested capital, and other purposes. These decisions have also found other uses of toll revenues—such as operating public transportation facilities—to be appropriate. In 1987, Congress in effect codified these decisions and repealed provisions that had expressly limited the use of toll revenues to specific purposes, such as maintaining, repairing, and operating a bridge. Key federal administrative and court decisions applying the "just and reasonable" standard are discussed in greater detail in Appendix II.

Bi-State Authorities Are Generally Not Subject to Federal or State Requirements for Public Involvement and Provided the Public Limited Opportunities to Participate in Recent Toll-Setting Decisions

In general, bi-state authorities are not required to follow federal or generally applicable state requirements for involving and informing the public, such as open meeting and open records laws. Instead, they set their own policies, which may be less stringent than those that apply to federal agencies, states, and other organizations. In addition, none of the four interstate compacts we reviewed contains language establishing specific public involvement requirements for toll setting. We found four areas in their most recent toll increases in which the bi-state authorities provided the public limited opportunities to learn about and provide comment on toll proposals, in contrast to federal and state requirements for involving the public, as well as practices used by other tolling authorities. See appendix III for a detailed timeline of public involvement in the four bi-state authorities' most recent toll increases.

---

[22]See, e.g., *Wallach v. Brezenoff,* 930 F.2d 1070 (3d Cir. 1991); *Automobile Club of New York, Inc. v. Port Authority of New York and New Jersey,* 706 F. Supp. 264 (S.D.N.Y 1989).

The Bi-State Authorities Are Not Subject to Federal or Generally Applicable State Requirements for Public Involvement

The bi-state authorities told us that they are not subject to federal or generally applicable state requirements for informing the public. For example, federal regulations for public participation in transportation decisions require regional planning bodies, known as metropolitan planning organizations (MPOs), to provide adequate notice and time for public review and comment, hold public meetings at convenient and accessible locations and times, and demonstrate explicit consideration and response to public input received in making planning decisions.[23] In addition, each of the four states has established laws governing open meetings and records for public agencies that include requirements such as giving notice before holding public meetings, as well as submitting information to the state on the rationale for a toll increase, the financial position of the agency, and the purposes for which revenues will be used. According to bi-state authority officials, none of these generally applicable laws applies to the four bi-state authorities. However, New York and New Jersey have enacted reciprocal state statutes that require the PANYNJ to hold open meetings.[24]

In the absence of federal or state requirements, the bi-state authority officials reported that they have established their own general policies for public involvement, including making records publicly available and holding open board meetings. These internal policies, however, have been criticized for being less open or accessible than federal or state requirements. For example, in September 2011, the New York State Committee on Open Government found that the PANYNJ's freedom of information policy—which allows the public to request PANYNJ documents—and open meeting policy were more restrictive and provided less access than freedom of information and open meetings laws that apply to state agencies in New York.[25]

---

[23]GAO, *Metropolitan Planning Organizations: Options Exist to Enhance Transportation Planning Capacity and Federal Oversight*, GAO-09-868 (Washington, D.C.: Sept. 9, 2009).

[24]N.Y. Unconsol. Laws 6416-A; N.J. Stat. § 32:1-6.1

[25]The New York State Committee on Open Government is a unit in the New York Department of State that oversees and advises the government, public, and news media on Freedom of Information, Open Meetings, and Personal Privacy Protection Laws. On September 6, 2011, the Committee issued an advisory opinion stating that the PANYNJ's policies for open records and open meetings fall short of the requirements in New York's Freedom of Information and Open Meetings Laws.

In addition to federal and state laws for public participation, federal agencies and the Transportation Research Board, a non-government research organization for transportation practice and policy, have identified leading practices that transportation agencies could use to involve the public in decision-making.[26] In reviewing state and federal law and leading practices, we identified several practices used by transportation agencies that are subject to federal and state requirements that provide a useful way to assess whether the bi-state authorities are meeting expectations the public may have for accountability and transparency from public agencies. These practices include:

- establishing a documented process for public involvement in toll-setting decisions;

- requiring sufficient opportunities for public comment before approving toll proposals;

- providing key information to the public to support toll proposals; and

- summarizing public input for decision makers and the public before toll proposals are put to a vote for approval.

The Bi-State Authorities Provided the Public Limited Opportunities to Participate in Recent Toll-Setting Decisions

We found that the bi-state authorities' efforts to involve the public during their most recent toll increases were limited in comparison with requirements for state and local transportation agencies and leading practices to involve the public in decision-making. The bi-state authorities did not in all cases (1) have documented public involvement processes for toll-setting; (2) provide the public with key information on their toll proposals in advance of public hearings; (3) offer the public sufficient opportunities to comment on toll proposals; and (4) provide a public summary of comments received before toll increases were approved.

Documented Process for Involving the Public in Toll Setting

According to the Transportation Research Board, establishing a defined, structured, and transparent process for involving the public in key decisions, such as those related to setting tolls, allows the public to

---

[26]Transportation Research Board of the National Academies, *Effective Public Involvement Using Limited Resources*, National Cooperative Highway Research Program Synthesis 407 (Washington, D.C.: 2010). Also see FHWA, *Public Involvement Techniques for Transportation Decision-Making*, Publication No.FHWA-PD-96-031 (Washington, D.C.: Dec. 1996).

understand the process and be aware of critical decision points where they can have influence if a toll increase is announced.[27] At the time of their most recent toll increases, the four bi-state authorities had general policies for holding open board meetings, but these policies did not outline specific steps for involving the public in toll increases. We have previously reported that having a transparent process for reviewing and updating user fees, such as tolls, helps assure payers and other stakeholders that user fees are set fairly and accurately and are spent on intended purposes. Furthermore, soliciting stakeholder input is particularly important in cases where there is a monopoly supplier, where alternatives are limited and fees are not fully voluntary.[28] Because the public may have few alternatives to using the tolled crossings, having a transparent, documented process specific to toll setting could improve the public's understanding of how the tolls work and what activities they may fund.

The four bi-state authorities' general policies do not provide the public with information specific to the toll-setting process, including: (1) the number of toll hearings the authority will hold, along with locations; (2) the amount of time that will be available to the public to comment on the proposal before it is voted on; and (3) how the authority will use public comments in its decision-making process. In addition, three of the four bi-state authorities did not have policies that specified the amount of advance notice to the public before holding public toll hearings. Only the PANYNJ's policies specify the length of advance notice (10 days). In contrast, bridge authorities in Michigan are required under state law to hold three public hearings and provide advance notice with dates, times, and locations prior to any proposed toll increase to allow the public an opportunity to comment. A documented process for public involvement also demonstrates to the public and to credit-rating agencies that toll-setting is taking place within a predictable framework and could create institutional memory within the authorities for toll setting in the future. Without a documented process for public involvement, the public lacks a clear view of the bi-state authorities' decision-making process, which

---

[27] Transportation Research Board of the National Academies, Committee on Public Involvement, *State of the Practice: White Paper on Public Involvement* (Washington, D.C.: 2000).

[28] GAO, *Federal User Fees: A Design Guide*, GAO-08-386SP (Washington, D.C.: May 29, 2008).

could undermine the authorities' ability to win the public's support and secure necessary toll revenues.

In commenting on a draft of this report, the PANYNJ stated that its policy is to provide the public with the amount, purpose, and estimated revenues of the proposed toll increase 10 days before convening toll hearings, and that this policy constitutes a documented public involvement process. According to the PANYNJ, this policy was established in 1977 through a resolution passed by its board of commissioners. However, PANYNJ board resolutions and other PANYNJ rules and regulations are generally not available to the public through its web site.[29] Consequently, at the time of the September 2011 toll increase, the public lacked the information needed to understand whether the PANYNJ was following its public involvement policies and making its toll-setting decisions in a predictable framework. In June 2012, the PANYNJ incorporated its 1977 public involvement policy into its publicly available bylaws. While this policy will be in effect for future toll increases, we do not believe that the PANYNJ's policy can be considered a defined and structured process for involving the public in key decisions because the policy still does not specify the number of toll hearings, the amount of time to be made available for the public to comment, and how the authority will utilize public comments.

Opportunities for Public Comment

Federal regulations pertaining to public participation require MPOs to provide adequate public notice and time for public review and comment at key decision points, and to hold any public meetings at convenient and accessible locations and times.[30] As we have previously reported, the public is a key stakeholder in any tolling decision, and providing for stakeholder input may affect support for and acceptance of a fee and contribute to improved understanding about how the fees work and what activities they fund.[31] The four bi-state authorities provided the public limited opportunities to comment before toll proposals were put to a vote for approval. For example, the DRJTBC did not hold any public hearings to receive public comment before approving its 2011 toll increase during

---

[29]The PANYNJ general counsel stated that members of the public may request a copy of PANYNJ resolutions from the Office of the PANYNJ's Secretary.

[30]23 C.F.R. § 450.316.

[31]GAO-08-386SP.

an open board meeting.[32] The DRPA and the DRBA each held one hearing per state to receive comment before approving their respective toll increases in open board meetings. Prior to convening toll hearings, the DRBA discussed the need for its toll increase in several board meetings that were open to the public. The PANYNJ held ten hearings on a toll proposal in various locations, including an online forum; however, those hearings were held in a single day. In contrast, officials from the Blue Water Bridge Authority and Mackinac Bridge Authority in Michigan reported that they typically provide 30 days after public notice is given for comment on toll proposals before approving an increase. Further, officials from the Golden Gate Bridge, Highway and Transportation District stated that they engaged the public through meetings, hearings, open houses, and other outreach for about 8 months prior to its last increase. The Bay Area Toll Authority in California began the public involvement process for its toll increase more than 6 months before the proposal was implemented with three public meetings held in locations around the region.

Key Information to Support Toll Proposals in Advance of Public Hearings

According to state and federal requirements and leading practices, agencies should provide key information to the public in advance of a toll proposal to give the public the opportunity to understand the agency's rationale for a toll increase and provide meaningful input to the decision-making process. However, the three bi-state authorities that held public toll hearings provided only limited information such as short descriptions of the capital projects they intended to implement using revenue from their proposed toll increases. The PANYNJ reported that at the time of its most recent toll proposal, it had not made a long-term capital plan available to the public detailing the full uses of the proposed toll and fare increases for the public to review. In prior work, we found that leading organizations prepare long-term capital plans that usually cover a 5- to 10-year period to document specific planned projects, plan for resource use, and establish priorities for implementation, and those plans are updated on an annual or biennial basis.[33]

---

[32]The DRJTBC reported that it did not hold toll hearings for its 2011 toll increase in which it raised passenger vehicle tolls to $1.00 because that toll rate remains less than a previously approved toll increase to $1.25 which was implemented in 2001. The DRJTBC reduced it to $.75 in 2003.

[33]GAO, *Executive Guide: Leading Practices in Capital Decision-Making*, GAO/AIMD-99-32 (Washington, D.C.: December 2008).

The PANYNJ reported that the June 2012 policy changes to its bylaws give the public information on the purposes for which tolls and fares are being adjusted and an estimate of the overall increase in revenues resulting from the change at least 10 days prior to holding public toll hearings. However, this policy is less stringent than a requirement applicable to state tolling authorities in New York, which must provide the governor, state comptroller, and legislators a special report supporting the proposed toll increase at least 120 days in advance. This report must include the authority's operation, debt service, and capital construction costs for the next 5 years, as well as estimates of the impact that revenues from the toll increase will have on the authority. Similarly, the public notice for the Golden Gate Bridge, Highway and Transportation District's 2010 toll increase proposal included information on its budget shortfall and need for new revenue, the proposed toll schedule and dates of implementation, revenues anticipated from the increase, and a comparison of the District's toll rates with similar bridge authorities around the country. Additionally, the Transportation Research Board has reported that those who are proactive in providing information are better able to guide public dialogue about the authority and its activities.[34]

Summary of Public Input for Decision Makers and the Public

According to the Transportation Research Board, one goal of a good public involvement process in transportation decisions is the incorporation of citizen input into decision making.[35] Providing the public the opportunity to voice its opinion on toll increases is important, and the ideas, preferences, and recommendations contributed by the public should be documented and seriously considered by decision makers. Additionally, federal regulations require that MPOs demonstrate explicit consideration and response to public input received during the transportation planning process.[36] Final toll-setting decisions should be communicated to the public with a description of how public input was considered and used.[37] According to the Transportation Research Board, a decision-making

---

[34]Transportation Research Board of the National Academies, *Public Participation Strategies for Transit*, Transit Cooperative Research Program Synthesis 89 (Washington, D.C.: 2011).

[35]Transportation Research Board, *State of the Practice: White Paper on Public Involvement* (2000).

[36]23 C.F.R. § 450.316 (a)(1)(vi).

[37]Institute for Local Government, *Principles of Local Government Public Engagement* (Sacramento, CA: June 10, 2010).

process that has public involvement inputs but no clear effect on the outputs is not a successful program.[38]

Only one of the four bi-state authorities created a summary of public input received during toll hearings and made it available to decision makers and the public. The PANYNJ provided a report to its commissioners summarizing the oral comments received at each of its ten public hearings, as well as written comments submitted, and made a transcript of each hearing publicly available on its website. After receiving public comment, the PANYNJ received a letter from the governors of New York and New Jersey voicing their disapproval of the initial increase, and modified its toll proposal to provide for more gradual toll increases over several years. The Mackinac Bridge Authority in Michigan also prepares a summary of public comments it receives at each hearing that categorizes responses according to those in favor of and opposed to the toll increase. This analysis distills the viewpoints of the public into a format that is readily useful to decision makers. Without evidence that decision-makers are considering the public's input before voting, the public lacks an assurance that its participation affects the tolling decision.

The Transportation Research Board has found that ongoing two-way communication is essential to a good public involvement program and that successful strategies provide continuous opportunities for the public to learn about and engage in the process.[39] Organizations that maintain an ongoing conversation with the public through the media, open houses, and outreach efforts may improve the public's buy-in and understanding of toll increases and how revenues will be used. Officials from the Golden Gate Bridge, Highway and Transportation District reported that regardless of whether a toll increase is being considered, engaging with the media regularly to discuss maintenance and capital projects is important so that the public is continually aware of the needs of the Golden Gate Bridge and how toll revenue is being used. By engaging the public in an ongoing conversation on how toll revenues are put to use, bi-state authorities have an opportunity to make a more convincing and transparent case for their toll proposals to secure necessary revenues.

---

[38]Transportation Research Board, *State of the Practice: White Paper on Public Involvement* (2000).

[39]Transportation Research Board, *State of the Practice*, 5.

External Oversight of Bi-State Tolling Authorities Has Been Limited, but Bi-State Authorities Have Established Some Internal Oversight

States Have Conducted Few Audits of Bi-State Tolling Authorities, and States' Audit Authorities Are Unclear

The external oversight of the bi-state authorities has been limited as only one of the four bi-state authorities has been regularly audited by a state audit entity. Specifically, the Office of the New York State Comptroller has conducted three audits of the PANYNJ in the past 5 years. The New Jersey Office of the State Comptroller conducted an investigation of the DRPA at the request of the governors of New Jersey and Pennsylvania in 2010, and with the approval of the DRPA board. Neither the DRJTBC nor the DRBA has been subject to an audit by state audit entities in their respective states. New Jersey State Comptroller and New Jersey State Auditor officials stated that they have authority to audit the four state bi-state authorities, but have not prioritized further audits of the authorities due to limited staffing resources and competing demands, such as auditing state agencies that receive state funds.

The few audits conducted have identified areas of concern in two bi-state tolling authorities. For example, in its July 2011 report on the PANYNJ's use of consulting, construction management, and other contracted services, the New York State Comptroller found that the PANYNJ lacked supporting documentation for 57 of the 75 contracts it reviewed, with a total value of $1.18 billion in contracts lacking justification that the services were needed.[40] Although the New York State Comptroller made several recommendations to improve the transparency of PANYNJ contracting, the PANYNJ does not have the same requirements as New York state agencies to report its progress in implementing recommendations, and it has not done so for this audit. As a result, the

---

[40]Office of the New York State Comptroller, *Port Authority of New York and New Jersey: Contracts for Personal and Miscellaneous Services*, Report 2009-S-54 (A bany, New York: July 19, 2011).

status of any actions taken by the PANYNJ to address the New York State Comptroller's recommendations is not publicly available. New York State Comptroller officials stated that in May 2013 it initiated a follow-up audit of the PANYNJ's contracting procedures in which it will report on the status of any reforms taken by the PANYNJ.

The New Jersey State Comptroller's investigation found that the DRPA did not follow its own policies for approving and monitoring economic development projects and raised questions as to whether selected projects were properly vetted.[41] The report also found that insurance brokers in New Jersey and Pennsylvania shared more than $1.5 million in commissions from the purchase of DRPA insurance policies, regardless of whether the brokers actually placed the policies "or performed any service at all." Although the sharing of insurance commissions is legal in New Jersey, the report noted that the practice was potentially wasteful of toll-payer funds. In response, the DRPA has adopted new competitive procurement policies to select insurance brokers to reduce the potential waste of toll-payer revenues. DRPA officials also reported that the board passed a resolution in August 2010 that prohibited the use of DRPA revenues for projects that are not directly connected to the assets under the board's direct control; however, another resolution in December 2011 permitted the allocation of DRPA's remaining economic development funds to complete seven economic development projects.

The authority of state audit agencies to oversee the bi-state authorities is in many cases unclear.[42] Prior work by GAO and others has found that audit authorities should be clearly established to ensure that those authorities are widely understood by the agencies responsible for oversight and among the communities they oversee.[43] However, differences in states' laws and disagreements between the bi-state authorities and the state audit agencies have prompted questions about

---

[41]New Jersey Office of the State Comptroller, *Investigative Report: Delaware River Port Authority* (Trenton, NJ: Mar. 29, 2012).

[42]Because this is a discussion of state law, we are not providing an independent analysis as to whether these laws establish audit authority over the bi-state authorities.

[43]See GAO, *United Nations: Status of Internal Oversight Services*, GAO/NSIAD-98-9 (Washington, D.C.: Nov. 19, 1997); also see International Organization of Supreme Audit Institutions, *General Standards in Government Auditing and Standards with Ethical Significance*, ISSAI 200 (Vienna, Austria: 2001).

the authority of several states to provide oversight. Some of the states with bi-state tolling authorities have similar, but not identical legislation pertaining to their audit authorities, and some could not point to any concurring language in their state laws.[44] For example, New Jersey State Comptroller officials stated that the office has standing authority to provide oversight of each of the bi-state tolling authorities under the New Jersey state law that enables it to audit New Jersey public agencies and independent state authorities.[45] The New Jersey State Auditor—a separate office from the New Jersey State Comptroller—also reported that its office has standing authority to audit the four bi-state authorities under a separate New Jersey state law.[46] Nonetheless, officials in both offices could not point to reciprocal legislation in Delaware and Pennsylvania establishing their authorities in those states.

In some cases, state audit agencies and bi-state authorities expressed disagreements over the extent of the state's audit authority, or stated that audit authority was not established. Specifically, New Jersey State Auditor officials reported that the office attempted to initiate an audit of the DRJTBC in July 2013, but the DRJTBC rejected the request stating in a letter that the audit was not authorized by the DRJTBC interstate compact or by state laws in New Jersey and Pennsylvania. DRJTBC officials also stated that the New Jersey State Comptroller does not have standing audit authority. In addition, the Delaware Office of Auditor of Accounts reported that it does not have the authority to audit the DRBA, and the Pennsylvania Auditor General reported that it does not have the authority to audit the DRPA and the DRJTBC. The DRBA and the DRPA took no position as to whether New Jersey or the other states have standing audit authority. Appendix IV provides additional information about oversight authorities for the four bi-state authorities in the four states.

In addition to state audit agencies, other state agencies may also have limited authority to review the activities of bi-state authorities. In one case

[44]Some compacts include language that enables states to modify the compact through reciprocal legislation. The DRPA, PANYNJ, and DRBA compacts include this type of language, while the DRJTBC compact does not. See *Int'l Union of Operating Eng'rs, Local 542 v. Del. River Joint Toll Bridge Comm.*, 311 F3d 273 (3d Cir. 2002) for a discussion of how various courts have interpreted this type of language.

[45]N.J. Stat. § C52:15C.

[46]N.J. State § C52:24-4.

we found that these limits posed risks to the accountability of federal transportation programs because the federal government lacked assurance that credits claimed by New Jersey to waive federal-aid matching fund requirements were in fact eligible and accurate. Under the federal-aid highway program, which provides about $40 billion annually to states to build and improve highways and bridges, states are typically required to provide a 20-percent funding match. However, a state may receive "toll credits" to reduce its matching requirement if it can demonstrate that toll revenues were spent on facility improvements and met other requirements.[47] According to FHWA officials, from fiscal year 2008 through 2011, FHWA approved over $334 million in federal toll credits from the four bi-state tolling authorities.[48] New Jersey applied these toll credits and others earned from other tolling authorities in the state to eliminate the state's entire required match for highway and transit projects from fiscal year 2008 through 2011.[49] FHWA officials in New Jersey stated that they rely on the state to self-certify the accuracy and eligibility of its own toll credits. However, New Jersey Department of Transportation (NJDOT) officials stated that NJDOT does not request or review underlying project documentation, such as contract awards or project schedules, from the bi-state authorities to support their eligibility certifications. NJDOT officials stated that they would have authority to conduct audits and spot checks of the bi-state authorities but they could

---

[47]As provided by federal law, and contingent upon meeting certain requirements, a state may be permitted reduce the amount of funds it is required to contribute to receive federal surface transportation funds by claiming credit for toll revenues generated and used to build, improve, or maintain highways, bridges, or tunnels that serve the public purpose of interstate commerce. 23 U.S.C. §120(j).

[48]New Jersey was the only state in our review that claimed toll credits for expenditures made by the bi-state tolling authorities in the past 5 fiscal years. According to FHWA officials, from fiscal year 2008 through 2011, New Jersey requested about $342 million in toll credits based on bi-state tolling authority expenditures. FHWA approved almost $1.8 billion in toll credits from four other tolling authorities in the state which are not bi-state entities, including the New Jersey Turnpike Authority, Burlington County Bridge Commission, Cape May County Bridge Commission, and the South Jersey Transportation Authority. Overall, FHWA has approved more than $7 billion in toll credits to New Jersey since the program was put in place in 1992; and New Jersey maintains a balance of approximately $3.2 billion in approved but unused toll credits as of August 2012 that can be used to eliminate its matching requirements in future years.

[49]From 2008 through 2011, NJDOT applied an average of almost $150 million in toll credits for highway projects, and New Jersey Transit applied an average of almost $90 million per year in toll credits for transit projects to eliminate the state matching requirements for those years.

not provide any documentation to that effect. The officials also stated that NJDOT has never conducted an audit or spot-check of any of the bi-state authorities' expenditures to confirm their eligibility for toll credits. As a result of states' limited oversight of bi-state tolling authorities, FHWA lacks assurance that the states are able to fully verify the information collected from the bi-state authorities before it is provided to FHWA for approval.

Officials from certain bi-state tolling authorities told us that the states exercise oversight through the governor's veto of the voting decisions of the commissioners from that state. This veto authority may provide an important check and balance on the boards' decisions with regard to the governors' priorities. However, such a veto power is limited to the voting decisions of the board and does not provide the public insight into the internal activities of the bi-state authorities that would otherwise be provided by an independent auditor. Moreover, this veto power is not always available to both governors. Specifically, according to DRJTBC and DRPA officials, the governor of Pennsylvania does not have veto authority over the DRJTBC or the DRPA because its state legislature has not provided that authority in state law.[50] According to the New Jersey Governor's office, New Jersey state law provides that the New Jersey Governor may veto actions of DRJTBC commissioners representing that state;[51] however, that authority has not been exercised because substantially similar legislation has not been passed in Pennsylvania. DRJTBC reported that the New Jersey Governor may not unilaterally enforce its veto authority without reciprocal legislation enacted in Pennsylvania, as well as an act of Congress to amend the compact.[52] In contrast, New Jersey and New York governors both have veto authority over the PANYNJ, and New Jersey and Delaware governors have veto authority over the DRBA.

---

[50]The DRPA reported that its compact provides that the state legislatures of New Jersey and Pennsylvania may establish a veto authority for each governor over the decisions of the commissioners appointed from his or her state. The New Jersey governor has veto authority over its DRPA commissioners and, according to a DRPA official, has recently exercised that authority to encourage revisions to DRPA resolutions on open meetings and open records.

[51]N.J. Stat. § 32:8-15.6-15.8.

[52]House Bills 619 and 621 have been introduced in the Pennsylvania General Assembly, which would provide the Pennsylvania governor the authority to veto certain actions of DRJTBC Pennsylvania Commissioners.

Bi-State Tolling Authorities Have Established Internal Oversight Mechanisms, but One Internal Audit Entity Lacks Assurance of Independence

Each of the four interstate bi-state tolling authorities has established internal oversight mechanisms with responsibilities that vary based on the size and complexity of the organization. The four bi-state tolling authorities each have an audit committee comprised of board commissioners that is charged with activities such as overseeing the auditing and financial reporting processes of the authority, coordinating external financial or management audits, and directing the activities of internal audit departments, if applicable. For example, every 2 years DRPA's audit committee selects an independent firm to conduct a management performance audit of DRPA business activities, which is intended to enhance transparency and enable the DRPA to more quickly identify issues that require the attention of the board and management. DRJTBC officials reported that the audit committee coordinates the annual audit of its financial statements and directs the auditors to perform stress tests of various functional areas, including management controls.

In addition to the activities of the audit committees, the two largest authorities, the PANYNJ and the DRPA, have also established separate inspectors general and internal audit departments that conduct their own performance and financial audits and respond to public or internal allegations of waste, fraud, and abuse. In general, internal audit entities are organizations that are accountable to senior management and those charged with governance of the audited entity.[53] Internal audit entities typically follow audit procedures and practices based on the standards established by the Institute of Internal Auditors,[54] and they are generally not subject to the standards that guide federal or state external auditors or inspectors general. For example, they do not generally report the results of their work to the public, Congress, or to their state's legislature.[55] However, like external audit agencies, internal audit entities are expected to be free from impairments to their independence and must avoid the appearance of any impairment to independence to meet professional auditing standards.[56]

---

[53]GAO-12-331G.

[54]Institute of Internal Auditors, *International Standards for the Professional Practice of Internal Auditing* (2012).

[55]GAO-07-1021T.

[56]See GAO-12-331G; also see IIA, *International Standards for the Professional Practice of Internal Auditing* (2012); and see GAO-07-1021T.

Although auditor independence is required by professional internal auditing standards, the DRPA has yet to establish clear access authorities for its inspector general. As a result, the DRPA office of inspector general lacks an assurance of independence. DRPA officials reported that the DRPA inspector general's office was established in 2012 in response to a 2010 bill introduced in the House of Representatives that called for Congress to withdraw its consent from DRPA's interstate compact if certain reforms, including creating the position, were not made.[57] However, the DRPA resolution establishing the inspector general did not establish authorities for it to access DRPA records and personnel, and according to DRPA officials, such written authorities did not exist at the time of our review. The DRPA inspector general reported that he had drafted standard operating procedures for his office based on standards for state or local inspectors general, which included audit authorities and oversight responsibilities, and submitted those procedures to DRPA's audit committee for its review.[58] Although the DRPA inspector general maintains that he does not need the board's approval for these standard operating procedures, the inspector general reported that members of the DRPA board attempted to weaken the authorities, including inserting a provision to require that the inspector general report any potential criminal activity to DRPA management rather than directly to legal authorities. The DRPA inspector general reported that he would not abide by this provision if enacted by the DRPA board. We requested from DRPA a copy of the standard operating procedures prepared by the inspector general; however, DRPA officials stated that these procedures have not been approved by the board and did not make them available for our review. As a result, we were unable to verify whether the authorities pursued by the DRPA inspector general were sufficient to enable the office to independently conduct its oversight responsibilities. In addition, the DRPA and PANYNJ declined our request to meet independently with officials from their respective inspectors general and internal audit departments without DRPA and PANYNJ management officials present.

By design, internal audit entities do not generally publically report their findings, and thus the public is usually not aware of the accountability

---

[57]H.R. 6202, 111th Cong. (2010).

[58]According to the DRPA IG, its draft operating procedures are based on the *Principles and Standards for Offices of Inspector General* prepared by the Association of Inspectors General.

efforts taken by these entities. For example, in 2011 the PANYNJ's internal audit department office completed 271 audits of PANYNJ activities and reported $12.9 million in estimated savings as a result of its audits. However, the PANYNJ audit department does not publically report findings. While the PANYNJ provided us with summaries of several audit reports, it declined our request to provide selected full audit reports for our review. DRPA's inspector general reported that it has conducted several audits and investigations and has released one report to the public. Although the Institute of Internal Auditors standards do not require internal audit departments to report audit results to the public, by not doing so, the public may be unaware of the efforts taken by bi-state authorities to safeguard toll payer revenues and improve management performance and operations.

Concluding Observations

Congress has given wide latitude to four states to address infrastructure needs in the Northeast by consenting to the creation of bi-state tolling authorities that operate some of the most highly traveled interstate crossings in the United States. These public authorities have broad authority to manage their operations without the same constraints, requirements, and oversight to which state and federal agencies are subject. Because these authorities are neither federal nor state entities, and because GAO does not make recommendations to non-federal entities, we are not making any recommendations in this report. The bi-state tolling authorities have recognized that the traveling public pays for these facilities, and that they must be accountable to the public. However, issues of transparency and accountability could undermine the authorities' ability to win the public's support and secure necessary toll revenues. As such, states have both the incentive and the opportunity to enhance the transparency and accountability of the bi-state tolling authorities.

Specifically, the bi-state tolling authorities would benefit from clear and consistent requirements for public involvement in decision-making to ensure a documented process for public involvement and meaningful and sufficient opportunities for the public to comment, among other measures. In addition, the states have the incentive to work together to clarify the lines of external oversight over the bi-state tolling authorities, so that each state's audit entity has sufficient standing authority and access to conduct audits and investigations of the operations of the bi-state tolling authorities. Furthermore, the internal audit entities of the bi-state tolling authorities are uniquely positioned to provide ongoing oversight and accountability. The DRPA established its inspector general in response to congressional concerns, and has the opportunity to more fully address those concerns by assuring the independence of its inspector general by establishing clear authorities for it to perform its work.

Agency Comments and Our Evaluation

We submitted a draft of this report to the DOT and the four bi-state tolling authorities for review and comment. The DOT and the DRPA had no comments on the draft. We received technical comments from the DRBA, the DRJTBC, and the PANYNJ, and we incorporated those comments as appropriate. We also provided sections of the draft report relating to the external oversight of the bi-state tolling authorities to state audit agencies in Delaware, New Jersey, New York, and Pennsylvania and received technical comments, which we incorporated as appropriate.

In addition to providing technical comments, the PANYNJ disagreed with our finding that it did not have a documented and structured public involvement process for setting tolls. The PANYNJ stated that its policy of providing 10-days advance notice before convening toll hearings and providing the public with the amount and purpose of proposed toll rates constituted a documented public involvement process. According to the PANYNJ, this policy was established in 1977 through a resolution passed by its board of commissioners. However, PANYNJ board resolutions and its other rules and regulations are generally not available to the public. Consequently, at the time of the September 2011 toll increase, the public lacked the information needed to understand the PANYNJ's public involvement policy, and whether the PANYNJ was following that policy and making its toll-setting decisions in a predictable framework. In June 2012, the PANYNJ incorporated its 1977 policy into its publicly available by-laws. While this policy will be in effect for future toll increases, we do not believe that it can be considered a defined and structured process for involving the public in key decisions because, as stated in our report, the policy does not specify the number of toll hearings, the amount of time to be made available for the public to comment, and how the authority will utilize public comments. The PANYNJ also disagreed with our finding that it did not offer the public sufficient opportunities to comment during its most recent toll increase, and stated that as a matter of practice, it has held multiple toll hearings in both states prior to toll increases. Our draft report recognized that the PANYNJ held 10 hearings in various locations for its proposed 2011 toll increase, including an online forum. However, because those hearings were held in a single day—and only 3 days prior to the board of commissioners' vote to approve toll increases—we believe that the accelerated schedule did not provide sufficient, convenient and accessible opportunities for the public to comment on the proposal.

As agreed with your offices, unless you publicly announce the contents of this report earlier, we plan no further distribution until 30 days from the report date. At that time, we will send copies of this report to congressional committees with responsibilities for surface transportation issues and the Secretary of Transportation. In addition, this report will be available at no charge on GAO's website at http://www.gao.gov.

If you or your staff have any questions about this report, please contact me at (202) 512-2834 or flemings@gao.gov. Contact points for our Offices of Congressional Relations and Public Affairs may be found on the last page of this report. GAO staff that made significant contributions to this report are listed in appendix V.

Sincerely yours,

Susan Fleming
Director, Physical Infrastructure Issues

Appendix I: Objectives, Scope, and Methodology

Our three objectives were to assess: (1) the authority of bi-state tolling authorities to set and use tolls and the factors that influence toll setting, (2) the extent to which bi-state tolling authorities involve and inform the public in their toll-setting decisions, and (3) the extent to which bi-state tolling authorities are subject to external and internal oversight.

To assess the authority of bi-state tolling authorities to set and use tolls and the factors that influence toll setting, we reviewed the interstate compacts of the four bi-state tolling authorities: the Port Authority of New York and New Jersey (PANYNJ), the Delaware River Port Authority (DRPA), the Delaware River and Bay Authority (DRBA), and the Delaware River Joint Toll Bridge Commission (DRJTBC). We also interviewed bi-state tolling authority officials for their perspectives of the key drivers that influence their tolling decisions. We corroborated testimonial evidence by (1) reviewing of the bi-state tolling authorities' most recent financial statements and annual reports, as well as recent official statements and related documentation provided by the bi-state tolling authorities; and (2) by interviewing credit rating agency officials and reviewing information that evaluates the financial standing of the bi-state tolling authorities. To assess the purposes for which toll revenues can be used, we reviewed the interstate compact agreements, including any amendments, and interviewed authority officials on their permitted use of toll revenues. We reviewed the allowable uses for toll revenues, but due to ongoing litigation between the PANYNJ and the American Automobile Association regarding recent toll increases by the PANYNJ, we did not assess the specific purposes and projects for which the PANYNJ uses its toll revenues. For consistency, we did not assess the specific purposes and projects for which the other bi-state authorities use their toll revenues. To determine the extent to which bi-state tolling authorities are influenced by the federal requirement that tolls be just and reasonable, we interviewed bi-state tolling authority officials and reviewed the federal "just and reasonable" standard for evaluating toll increases, in section 508 of title 33, U.S. Code and conducted a legal review of how this standard has been interpreted and enforced by federal courts and federal agencies. The results of our legal review are provided in appendix II.

To assess the extent to which the bi-state tolling authorities involve and inform the public in their toll-setting decisions, we interviewed officials from each of the bi-state authorities regarding their efforts to involve the public in recent toll increases. We also reviewed documentation on each authority's most recent toll increase—such as public notices, newspaper articles, meeting minutes, board resolutions, and official statements—as provided by the authorities and collected from their public websites. We

also examined the bi-state authorities' interstate compacts and bylaws to
determine whether their policies for public involvement met several
practices that incorporate federal and state requirements for involving the
public, as well as practices used by other tolling authorities. These
practices include: (1) establishing a documented process for public
involvement, (2) requiring sufficient opportunities for public comment, (3)
providing key information to the public, and (4) summarizing public
comments. We selected these practices through analysis of federal
requirements for public participation by metropolitan planning
organizations, state laws for public involvement in tolling decisions,
guidance on involving the public in transportation decisions from the
Transportation Research Board, and our previous work on designing user
fees.[1] We also interviewed officials from five bridge toll authorities in
California and Michigan that were not created by interstate compacts
regarding their efforts to involve and inform the public in recent toll-setting
decisions. We selected these authorities because they manage and
operate tolled bridges that are similar in scale to the bi-state authorities,
have similar governance structures, and recently implemented a toll
increase.

To assess the extent to which bi-state tolling authorities are subject to
external and internal oversight, we reviewed available audit reports and
interviewed and collected information from the state audit agencies of
each of the four charter states in our review (New Jersey, New York,
Pennsylvania, and Delaware) and from the audit organizations within the
bi-state tolling authorities. To assess external oversight, we reviewed the
results of recent audits and investigations of the bi-state tolling
authorities, including an investigation of DRPA completed by the New
Jersey Office of the State Comptroller in 2012, and several audits of the
PANYNJ conducted by the Office of the New York State Comptroller. We
also reviewed relevant state laws in New Jersey, New York, and

---

[1]See 23 C.F.R. § 450.316. See also Transportation Research Board of the National
Academies, *Effective Public Involvement Using Limited Resources,* National Cooperative
Highway Research Program Synthesis 407 (Washington, D.C.: 2010); Transportation
Research Board of the National Academies, Committee on Public Involvement in
Transportation Planning, *State of the Practice: White Paper on Public Involvement*
(Washington, D.C.: 2000); FHWA, *Public Involvement Techniques for Transportation
Decision-Making*, Publication No.FHWA-PD-96-031 (Washington, D.C.: Dec. 1996);
Institute for Local Government, *Principles of Local Government Public Engagement*
(Sacramento, CA: June 10, 2010); and GAO, *Federal User Fees: A Design Guide,*
GAO-08-386SP (Washington, D.C. May 29, 2008).

Pennsylvania regarding the oversight of the bi-state tolling authorities in
those states and we interviewed officials with the New Jersey Office of
the State Comptroller, the New Jersey State Auditor, the Office of the
New York State Comptroller, the Pennsylvania Department of the Auditor
General, and the Delaware Office of Auditor of Accounts in order to
describe statutory audit authorities pertaining to the bi-state tolling
authorities. Because this is a discussion of state law, we are not providing
an independent analysis as to whether these laws establish audit
authority over the bi-state authorities. To assess the internal oversight of
the bi-state authorities, we collected information on the internal audit
mechanisms in place in each of the bi-state tolling authorities and we
interviewed the officials from the offices of the inspector general within the
PANYNJ and DRPA. We compared the external oversight structure with
GAO's *Government Auditing Standards* and other relevant GAO work on
oversight of non-federal entities,[2] and we compared the activities of the
internal audit entities with the *International Standards for the Professional
Practice of Internal Auditing* published by the Institute of Internal Auditors
and related GAO work on internal auditing.[3]

We conducted this performance audit from July 2012 through August
2013 in accordance with generally accepted government auditing
standards. Those standards require that we plan and perform the audit to
obtain sufficient, appropriate evidence to provide a reasonable basis for
our findings and conclusions based on our audit objectives. We believe
that the evidence obtained provides a reasonable basis for our findings
and conclusions based on our audit objectives.

---

[2]GAO, *Government Auditing Standards: 2011 Revision*, GAO-12-331G (Washington,
D.C.: Dec. 2011); International Organization of Supreme Audit Institutions, *General
Standards in Government Auditing and Standards with Ethical Significance*, ISSAI 200
(Vienna, Austria: 2001); GAO, *Inspectors General: Proposals to Strengthen Independence
and Accountability*, GAO-07-1021T (Washington, D.C.: Jun. 20, 2007); GAO, *United
Nations: Status of Internal Oversight Services*, GAO/NSIAD-98-9 (Washington, D.C.: Nov.
19, 1997).

[3]The Institute of Internal Auditors, *International Standards for the Professional Practice of
Internal Auditing*, (Altamonte Springs, FL: Oct. 2012); GAO/NSIAD-98-9; GAO-07-1021T.

Appendix II: Discussion of the Federal "Just and Reasonable" Standard and Significant Federal Administrative and Court Decisions Addressing Toll Increase Challenges

In order to describe the current federal oversight environment, we provide this summary of the development of the just and reasonable standard for setting tolls on bridges, of significant federal administrative and court decisions interpreting it, and of whether courts have found there is a private right of action to enforce it. In addition, we discuss several cases challenging toll increases brought under the Commerce Clause of the U.S. Constitution.[1] As detailed below, the federal standard for the setting of bridge tolls by states—that tolls be "just and reasonable"—was established in federal law in 1906.[2] While the standard has remained unchanged to the present day, the federal government no longer has an oversight role in its implementation.[3] The Secretary of War initially had responsibility for enforcing the standard, and this responsibility was transferred to the Secretary of Transportation in 1968, where it remained until the Department of Transportation's (DOT) oversight authority was repealed in 1987. Since that time, a handful of lawsuits have been filed in the federal courts in effect seeking to enforce the just and reasonable standard. Rather than addressing what that standard means, however, most of these cases have grappled with who has the right to enforce it, that is, whether the statute creates a "private right of action" for private individuals or entities to bring suit to enforce the standard. The U.S. Court of Appeals for the Third Circuit has ruled that the statute does not provide a private right of action.[4] The U.S. Court of Appeals for the Second Circuit has issued a ruling applying the "just and reasonable" standard, but did not address whether a private right of action to enforce the standard exists.[5] Lower federal courts have not formally decided the issue but have discussed it generally.[6] A few of these courts also analyzed a challenge to

---

[1]The Commerce Clause provides Congress with the power to "regulate Commerce... among the several states..." U.S. Const. art. I, § 8, cl. 3.

[2]Act of March 23, 1906, Ch. 113, § 4, 34 Stat. 85.

[3]The current requirement that tolls on bridges be just and reasonable is found at 33 U.S.C. § 508.

[4]*American Trucking Ass'n v. Delaware River Joint Toll Bridge Comm'n*, 458 F.3d 291 (3d Cir. 2006).

[5]*Automobile Club of New York, Inc. v. Port Authority of New York and New Jersey*, 887 F.2d 417 (2d Cir. 1989).

[6]*Molinari v. New York Triborough Bridge and Tunnel Auth.*, 838 F.Supp. 718 (E.D.N.Y. 1993); *Auto Club of New York, Inc. v. Port Auth. of New York and New Jersey*, 842 F. Supp.2d 672 (S.D.N.Y. 2012).

Appendix II: Discussion of the Federal "Just
and Reasonable" Standard and Significant
Federal Administrative and Court Decisions
Addressing Toll Increase Challenges

a toll increase using a Constitutional "dormant commerce clause analysis," which focuses on whether state taxation discriminates against or unduly burdens interstate commerce and thereby impedes free private trade in the national marketplace.[7] These cases are discussed in more detail below.

The Three Federal Bridge Statutes

The General Bridge Act of 1906 (1906 Act)[8] sought "to establish uniform regulations with regard to the construction and operation of bridges authorized by Congress."[9] The 1906 Act also authorized the Secretary of War to fix the rates of tolls and stated that:

> "[i]f tolls shall be charged for the transit over any bridge constructed under the provisions of said sections,...such tolls shall be reasonable and just and the Secretary of War may, at any time, and from time to time prescribe the reasonable rates of tolls for such transit over such bridge..."

It was not until 1926 that informal congressional guidance specified what was entailed in the "reasonable and just" standard. As articulated by key House and Senate members,[10] the standard meant that tolls for bridges should be limited to those necessary to provide a fund sufficient to pay for the cost of maintaining, repairing and operating the bridge, and to provide a sinking fund to amortize the cost of the bridge, including reasonable interest and financing costs, as soon as possible under reasonable charges. After the sinking fund had been provided, the bridge was to be operated toll-free or with tolls adjusted so as not to exceed its operating and maintenance costs. It would take another 20 years before these

---

[7] *Auto Club of New York, Inc. v. Port Auth. of New York and New Jersey,* 842 F. Supp. 2d 672 (S.D.N.Y. 2012).

[8] Act of March 23, 1906, Ch. 113, § 4, 34 Stat. 85.

[9] H.R. Rep. No. 59-182, at 1-2 (1906). See *A Study of Federal Statutes and Regulations Governing Toll Bridges*", U.S. Department of Transportation (July 1974).

[10] A new bridge policy was agreed to by members of the Senate Committee on Commerce and the House Committee on Interstate and Foreign Commerce as conveyed in statements made on the House and Senate floors. 67 Cong. Rec. 8531 (House—April 30, 1926); 67 Cong. Rec. 8572 (Senate—May 1, 1926).

principles were put into legislation under the General Bridge Act of 1946 (1946 Act).[11]

The Secretary of War issued very few decisions during the period he was responsible for overseeing and enforcing the 1906 and 1946 Acts. However, one of the more significant cases involved a complainant who argued that it was unjust and unreasonable to divert automobile users' tolls for the purpose of paying the costs of port development and improvements. The Secretary ruled against the complainant saying that because Congress had approved the bi-state compact establishing the Delaware River Port Authority, which authorized the Authority to pool revenues from all of its income-producing activities, and authorized the expenditure of revenues so pooled for port development and port promotion purposes, the Authority's decision to use toll revenues for those purposes was within its sound managerial discretion. Hence, the Secretary determined, the higher tolls could not be said to be unjust or unreasonable simply because they contributed to financing operations that did not directly benefit highway users.[12]

The duties for administering the 1906 and 1946 Acts were transferred to the Secretary of Transportation by the Department of Transportation Act of 1966.[13] In addition, the Secretary was given jurisdiction over international bridges in the International Bridge Act of 1972 (1972 Act).[14] The 1972 Act also included a "just and reasonable" clause where tolls could be collected for amortization of the construction or acquisition costs of the bridge, including interest and financing costs, and for earning a reasonable return on invested capital.[15]

---

[11]Act of August 2, 1946, Ch. 753, Title V, 60 Stat. 847.

[12]Camden Bridge Toll, Secretary of the Army, May 4, 1954.

[13]Pub. L. No. 89-670, 80 Stat. 931 (1966).

[14]Pub. L. No. 92-434, 86 Stat. 731 (1972).

[15]Pub. L. No. 92-434, §6(1), 86 Stat. 731 (1972).

Appendix II: Discussion of the Federal "Just
and Reasonable" Standard and Significant
Federal Administrative and Court Decisions
Addressing Toll Increase Challenges

Significant Federal Administrative and Court Decisions During DOT Oversight of Toll Increases from 1970-1987

From 1970 until 1987, the Federal Highway Administration (FHWA) Administrator, to whom the Secretary of Transportation delegated his toll-oversight authority,[16] determined whether bridge toll increases were "just and reasonable" under the 1906, 1946, and 1972 Acts. The first significant case in which a court reviewed FHWA's determinations occurred in 1973. The U.S. Court of Appeals for the Eighth Circuit, in the *Burlington v. Turner* case,[17] reviewed a decision of the Federal Highway Administrator that the toll structure set by the City of Burlington, Iowa for its toll bridge over the Mississippi River was unjust and unreasonable under the 1906 Act.[18] The court found that toll rates for the Macarthur Bridge between Iowa and Illinois should be limited to an amount sufficient to pay the reasonable cost of maintaining, repairing and operating the bridge and its approaches under economical management; to provide a sinking fund for amortization of the bridge indebtedness; and to provide a reasonable return on invested capital. In 1974, the year after the Burlington decision, the FHWA administrator, in the Keokuk Bridge Tolls case, applied the principles of the Burlington case and found that an 8 percent rate of return with added operating and maintenance expenses was reasonable. However, because half of the toll revenues went to municipal programs and projects unrelated to the bridge, the Administrator determined that the rates were not reasonable and just.[19] Then in 1979, the U.S. Court of Appeals for the Second Circuit, in *Automobile Club of New York v. FHWA*, 592 F. 2d 658 (2d Cir. 1979), upheld the decision of the FHWA Administrator and a lower court allowing inclusion of complementary capital improvements to highways or transit systems in the rate base for setting tolls for bridges for the Port Authority of New York and New Jersey (PANYNJ).

The 1987 Act and Significant Federal Court Decisions since Enactment

The Surface Transportation and Uniform Relocation Act Assistance Act of 1987 (1987 Act) repealed DOT's authority to review bridge toll increases, but maintained the requirement that tolls on bridges constructed under the authority of the 1906, 1946 and 1972 Acts must be "just and

[16]49 C.F.R. § 1.48(i), 35 Fed. Reg. 4960 (March 21, 1970).

[17]471 F.2d 120 (8th Cir. 1973).

[18]The FHWA decision was reviewed first by a district court, 336 F. Supp. 594 (S.D. Iowa 1972), where the action was brought pursuant to the Administrative Procedure Act.

[19]*In the Matter of Keokuk Bridge Tolls*, Federal Highway Administration, April 23, 1974.

reasonable."[20] The 1987 Act also repealed the 1946 Act's express limitation of the use of toll revenues to specific bridge-related purposes such as maintaining, repairing, and operating a bridge. Since DOT's authority for reviewing bridge toll increases was repealed in 1987, the federal courts have become the sole forum for challenges to tolls both under the statutory "just and reasonable" standard of the 1987 Act as well as under the Commerce Clause of the U.S. Constitution.[21] A handful of federal court cases have applied the "just and reasonable" standard and addressed whether private parties can bring suit to enforce it. As summarized below, courts in different circuits have reached different conclusions or expressed different views regarding whether private parties have the right to raise such challenges in court under the "just and reasonable" standard. This has not been an issue for those cases brought under the Commerce Clause.

(1) *Automobile Club of New York, Inc. v. Port Authority of New York and New Jersey*, 887 F. 2d 417 (2d Cir. 1989) – The central issue of this case was whether it was "just and reasonable" for the PANYNJ to include losses from the Port Authority Trans-Hudson (PATH) Railroad in the Port Authority's rate base for determining the tolls to be charged for passage over the bridges owned by the PANYNJ between New York and New Jersey. The plaintiffs contended that that the bridge toll increases violated both the statutory "just and reasonable" standard in the 1987 Act and the Constitution's Commerce Clause. The federal district court dismissed the "unjust and unreasonable" argument,[22] finding that the statutory standard had sufficient "flexibility" to allow inclusion of functionally-related but non-bridge (PATH) costs in the PANYNJ's rate base. The court also rejected the argument that including non-bridge costs in setting bridge tolls imposed an excessive and unconstitutional burden on interstate commerce, Applying a three-part test previously established by the Supreme Court,[23] the lower court found that (1) the challenged state action regulated evenhandedly, with only "incidental" effects on interstate

---

[20]Pub. L. No. 100-17, § 135, 101 Stat. 132, 174 (April 2, 1987). The just and reasonable requirement is codified at 33 U.S.C. § 508.

[21]The Commerce Clause provides Congress with the power to "regulate Commerce… among the several states…" U.S. Const. art. I, § 8, cl. 3.

[22]*Automobile Club of New York, Inc. v. Port Auth of New York and New Jersey*, 706 F. Supp. 264 (S.D.N.Y. 1989).

[23]*See Hughes v. Oklahoma*, 441 U.S. 322, 336 (1979).

Appendix II: Discussion of the Federal "Just
and Reasonable" Standard and Significant
Federal Administrative and Court Decisions
Addressing Toll Increase Challenges

commerce; (2) the state action served a legitimate local purpose; and (3) there were no alternative means to promote this local purpose that would not also affect interstate commerce. On appeal, the Second Circuit, in a 2-1 decision, upheld the lower court's ruling that PATH was sufficiently related to the PANYNJ's bridges and tunnels to warrant its inclusion in the rate base on which "just and reasonable" bridge tolls were based. The Commerce Clause challenge was not raised on appeal. Neither the district court nor the Court of Appeals, however, explicitly addressed the issue of whether the 1987 Act creates a private right of action.

(2) *Wallach v. Brezenoff*, 930 F. 2d 1070 (3d Cir. 1991) – In this case, New Jersey citizens brought suit against the PANYNJ challenging toll increases both under the "just and reasonable" standard found in the 1987 Act and the Commerce Clause. At the district court level, the court granted the PANYNJ's motion for summary judgment and the plaintiffs appealed solely based on the Commerce Clause issues. The Third Circuit court rejected the appeal by pointing to the reasons given by the district court in *Automobile Club of New York, Inc. v. Port. Auth. of New York and New Jersey*, 706 F. Supp. 264 (S.D.N.Y. 1989), i.e., that (1) the challenged state action regulated evenhandedly, with only "incidental" effects on interstate commerce; (2) the state action served a legitimate local purpose; and (3) there were no alternative means to promote this local purpose that would not also affect interstate commerce.

(3) *Molinari v. New York Triborough Bridge and Tunnel Authority*, 838 F.Supp. 718 (E.D.N.Y. 1993) – The plaintiffs in Molinari brought suit against the New York Triborough Bridge and Tunnel Authority, challenging the 1989 and 1993 toll increases on the Verrazano-Narrows Bridge. They maintained that the tolls were "unjust and unreasonable" within the meaning of the 1987 Act solely because they were used to subsidize the mass transportation components of the Metropolitan Transportation Authority. The district court granted the Authority's motion for summary judgment, finding that "plaintiffs have failed to create even a triable issue of fact on their claim that the challenged toll increases on the Verrazano-Narrows Bridge are unjust and unreasonable."[24] "[I]f a bridge toll generates more revenue than necessary to provide a fair profit or rate of return," the court continued, "the toll may not be challenged successfully if it is used to support a single integrated transportation

---

[24]838 F. Supp. 718, 724 (E.D.N.Y. 1993).

Appendix II: Discussion of the Federal "Just
and Reasonable" Standard and Significant
Federal Administrative and Court Decisions
Addressing Toll Increase Challenges

system in which the successful operation of the bridge is dependent in whole or in part on the operation of the other related facilities."[25] The court also raised serious questions regarding whether a private right of action exists under the 1987 Act, finding that not only does the statute not explicitly create such a right, it also lacks the kind of "right- or duty-creating language" that has generally been the most accurate indicator of the propriety of implication of a cause of action."[26] Finally, the court noted that the "Supreme Court has . . . been 'especially reluctant to imply causes of action under statutes [such as section 508 of the 1987 Act] that create duties on the part of persons for the benefit of the public at large"[27] and that there was a compelling case to be made that a private right of action should not be implied.[28]

(4) *American Trucking Association v. Delaware River Joint Toll Bridge Commission*, 458 F.3d 291 (3d Cir. 2006) – In this case, the U.S. Court of Appeals for the Third Circuit found that the 1987 Act's "just and reasonable" provision did not create a private right of action for truck drivers to challenge the reasonableness of tolls on bi-state bridges

---

[25]*Id.* at 725.

[26]*Id.* at 724.

[27]*Id.* at 724.

[28]Legislative history accompanying the 1987 Act shows that Congress was divided over how the "just and reasonable" standard was to be enforced following repeal of DOT's oversight responsibility. Senate reports accompanying two bills that preceded the 1987 Act and which contained language similar to that found in the 1987 Act (the Federal Aid Highway Act of 1984 and the Interstate Highway Funding Act of 1985) contained language indicating that the federal courts would be the proper forum for challenges pursuant to the 1987 Act's just and reasonable standard. Both reports stated that "[by] placing this requirement in the statute, the Committee has created a basis for which a user may commence suit in federal Court if he or she believes actions of a toll authority are not just and reasonable." See S. Rep. No. 98-524 (1984); S. Rep. No. 99-2 (1985). The Chairman of the House Committee on Public Works and Transportation stated, in regard to the Surface Transportation and Uniform Relocation Assistance Act of 1987, that "[the] only thing we have changed is the forum for making the determination. Toll increases will no longer be subject to review by the Department of Transportation; instead the decision will be left to the courts in the event of a challenge." Congressional Record, March 31, 1987. However, a section-by-section analysis of the bill stated that "State and toll authorities would be given greater flexibility in operating toll facilities. Federal oversight of the reasonableness of tolls has proven to be administratively burdensome, legally unproductive, and has interjected the Federal Government in the role of a mediator in disputes which could more appropriately be settled at the State and local level." Section-by-Section Analysis of S. 312—Essential Highway Reauthorization Amendments of 1987, 133 Cong. Rec. S778.

Appendix II: Discussion of the Federal "Just
and Reasonable" Standard and Significant
Federal Administrative and Court Decisions
Addressing Toll Increase Challenges

operated by the Delaware River Joint Toll Bridge Commission. The court ruled that the statute contained no language that might suggest a congressional desire to allow a private suit to enforce the "just and reasonable" provision. In the absence of explicit language conferring a private right of action, the court addressed whether a private right of action could be implied under the Supreme Court's four-factor test in *Cort v. Ash*: (1) does the statute create a federal right in favor of the particular plaintiff?; (2) is there any indication of legislative intent either to create such a remedy or to deny one?; (3) is it consistent with the underlying purposes of the legislative scheme to imply such a remedy for the particular plaintiff?; and (4) is the cause of action one traditionally relegated to state law so that it would be inappropriate to infer a cause of action based solely on federal law?[29] Under the Supreme Court's first factor, the Third Circuit found that the 1987 Act was designed to benefit the public at large, not truckers specifically. Under the second factor, the Third Circuit found legislative history on both sides of the issue and thus no clear expression of legislative intent that a private right of action was supported. This was sufficient for the court to find that there was no private right of action under the 1987 Act. The Court noted, as an aside, that the truckers had not raised any constitutional challenge in this case.

(5) *Auto Club of New York, Inc. v. Port Authority of New York and New Jersey*, 842 F. Supp. 2d 672 (S.D.N.Y. 2012) – In this case, the Auto Clubs of New York and New Jersey (together AAA) sought to halt toll increases proposed by the PANYNJ for its bridges and tunnels, arguing that they violated the Constitution's Commerce Clause and the just and reasonable standard of the 1987 Act. In particular, AAA argued that 2011 toll increases on PANYNJ bridges and tunnels which were earmarked to fund cost overruns in the PANYNJ's real estate development at the World Trade Center violated the statutory "just and reasonable" standard because the increases were not functionally related to the PANYNJ's integrated, interdependent transportation network and so should not have been included in the rate base. AAA also claimed the toll increases were unreasonable under the Constitution's so-called dormant Commerce Clause because the tolls were not "based on a fair approximation of…use" of the bridges and tunnels and are "excessive in

---

[29]*Cort v. Ash*, 422 U.S. 66 (1975).

relation to the benefits conferred" on the users.[30] AAA sought to stop the toll increases both temporarily—on an emergency basis—and permanently.

The district court rejected AAA's request for immediate relief to stop the toll increases, finding that AAA did not show, as required, that it would likely win the case when all the facts are heard (the case is still ongoing). The court stated that it did not need to reach the question of whether AAA had a private right of action under the 1987 Act. It did, however, raise questions about the Third Circuit's reasoning in the American Trucking case (discussed above) saying that it "leaves no means of enforcement [for the 1987 Act], making the words 'just and reasonable' mere surplusage and conflicting with the text and structure of the rest of the act."[31] The district court also questioned American Trucking's suggestion that "the state political process could be the venue that Congress had in mind for the airing of toll grievances" since one state's legislature cannot unilaterally modify tolls on a bi-state bridge without impinging on the rights of the other state's citizens in violation of the Commerce Clause. Further, the district court questioned the American Trucking court's use of legislative history to justify its decision, since it "waived away Committee reports from two earlier (but unpassed) versions of the Highway Act containing similar 'just and reasonable' language, reports which stated that 'the Committee has created a basis for which a user may commence a suit in Federal Court' upon belief 'that actions of a toll authority are not just and reasonable.'"[32]

The parties agreed that a 3-prong test applied by the Supreme Court in 1994[33] was applicable to determine the reasonableness of fees for the use of state-provided facilities by those engaged in interstate

---

[30]The courts have interpreted the Commerce Clause to include a "dormant Commerce Clause," meaning that by negative implication under the Clause, the federal government has power to "prohibit[] state taxation or regulation that discriminates against or unduly burdens interstate commerce and thereby impedes free private trade in the national marketplace." *See, e.g., Selevan v. New York Thruway Authority*, 584 F.3d 82 (2d Cir. 2009).

[31]842 F. Supp. 2d 672, 679 (S.D.N.Y. 2012).

[32]*Id.* at 679.

[33]*Northwest Airlines, Inc. v. County of Kent*, 510 U.S. 355 (1994).

commerce.[34] Under this test, a fee is reasonable, and thus constitutionally permissible, "if it (1) is based on some fair approximation of the use of the facilities, (2) is not excessive in relation to the benefits conferred, and (3) does not discriminate against interstate commerce."[35] Applying this test, the district court found that AAA failed to show it likely will succeed on either on its Commerce Clause claim or its claim under the Highway Act, even assuming a private right of action exists under the 1987 Act.

---

[34]The Commerce Clause provides Congress with the power to "regulate Commerce... among the several states..." U.S. Const. art. 1, § 8, cl. 3. From this federal grant of regulatory power flows the negative or dormant implication that the Commerce Clause "prohibits state taxation or regulation that discriminates against or unduly burdens interstate commerce and thereby impedes free private trade in the national marketplace."

[35] *Northwest Airlines*, above, 510 U.S. at 369, quoting *Evansville-Vanderburgh Airport Authority Dist. v. Delta Airlines, Inc.*, 405 U.S. 707 at 716-717.

Figure 1: Timeline of Public Involvement in Most Recent Toll Increases by Bi-state Tolling Authorities

PANYNJ

! August 5: The Port Authority of New York and New Jersey (PANYNJ) proposes toll and fare increases for its 6 crossings and commuter rail. Round-trip cash toll rate for passenger vehicles is $8.00.

ⓘ August 16: 10 public hearings (5 in NY, 4 in NJ, 1 online) to receive comment.

August 18: Governors of New York and New Jersey submit a letter to the PANYNJ disapproving of the proposed increase and provide an alternative proposal with the condition that the PANYNJ conduct a comprehensive management audit.

✓ August 19: PANYNJ board approves the governors' alternative toll and fare increase proposal.

$ September 18: First toll and fare increase takes effect, with additional increases scheduled for December 2012, 2013, 2014, and 2015. Current cash toll rate for passenger vehicles is $13.00.

DRJTBC

✓ May 2: The Delaware River Joint Toll Bridge Commission (DRJTBC) board approves a $0.25 increase in tolls on its 7 tolled bridges during its monthly open board meeting without toll hearings and issues press release announcing new toll rates. Cash toll rate for passenger vehicles is $0.75.

$ June 30: Toll increase takes effect. Current cash toll rate for passenger vehicles is $1.00.

DRBA

! April 19: The Delaware River and Bay Authority (DRBA) proposes a toll increase for the Delaware Memorial Bridge. Cash toll rate for passenger vehicles is $3.00.

ⓘ April 27-28: 2 public hearings in DE and NJ to receive comment.

✓ May 17: DRBA board approves proposed toll increase.

$ July 1: Toll increase on Delaware Memorial Bridge takes effect. Current cash toll rate for passenger vehicles is $4.00.

Jan	Feb	Mar	Apr	May	Jun	Jul	Aug	Sep	Oct	Nov	Dec

2011

DRPA

! July 10, 2008: The Delaware River Port Authority (DRPA) proposes toll and fare increases for its 4 bridges and commuter rail. Cash toll rate for passenger vehicles is $4.00.

ⓘ July 22-23, 2008: 2 public hearings in PA and NJ to receive comment.

✓ August 20, 2008: In response to public comment, DRPA board approves toll and fare increases in 2 phases for September 2008 and September 2010.

$ September 14, 2008: First toll and fare increase takes effect.

X December 9, 2009: DRPA board approves delay in second toll and fare increase.

$ July 1, 2011: Second toll and fare increase takes effect. Current cash toll rate for passenger vehicles is $5.00.

2008	2009	2010	2011

! Public notice of toll increase proposal
ⓘ Public hearing(s) held
✓ Board of Commissioners approves toll increase
X Board of Commissioners delays toll increase
$ Toll increase takes effect

Source: GAO analysis of bi-state tolling agency documentation.

Appendix IV: Summary of States' Reported Audit Authority over the Four Bi-state Tolling Authorities

Delaware River and Bay Authority (DRBA), New Jersey and Delaware[1]

Officials from the New Jersey Office of the State Comptroller stated that, the office, established in 2007, has standing oversight authority over DRBA—and the three other bi-state authorities—under the New Jersey state law that enables it to audit and investigate New Jersey "public agencies" and "independent state authorities."[2] However, it has not been firmly established in state law or state judicial cases that these bi-state authorities are considered "public agencies" or "independent state authorities" for the purposes of this law. The New Jersey State Auditor—a separate agency from the New Jersey Office of the State Comptroller—also reported that it has authority to audit the four bi-state tolling authorities under a New Jersey state law that provides for a performance audit of "any independent authority, or any public entity or grantee that receives state funds."[3] However, the New Jersey State Auditor also stated that receiving state funds is not necessarily a precondition for its audit authority over DRBA or any of the bi-state tolling authorities.[4]

Nonetheless, officials with the New Jersey Office of the State Comptroller and the New Jersey State Auditor were unaware of reciprocal legislation in Delaware recognizing their offices' audit authority over DRBA. The Delaware Office of the Auditor of Accounts stated that it does not have audit authority over DRBA because it is not a state agency and does not receive state funds. Neither New Jersey nor Delaware has audited DRBA. DRBA officials took no position as to whether either state had standing audit authority, but stated that DRBA would entertain a request for audit if contacted by either state auditor. Although the New Jersey Office of the State Comptroller has not been refused access by any of these entities there remains an open question as to the applicability of these provisions to these bi-state authorities.

---

[1]Because this is a discussion of state law, we are not providing an independent analysis as to whether these laws establish audit authority over the bi-state authorities.

[2]N.J. Stat. § C52:15C.

[3]N.J. State § C52:24-4.

[4]New Jersey State Auditor officials reported that the DRBA has received almost $1.7 million in New Jersey state funds since fiscal year 2003, primarily for ferry and airport projects, and that the Delaware River Port Authority is the only other bi-state tolling authority that has received funds from the State of New Jersey—less than $1 million since fiscal year 2004 primarily for emergency services.

Delaware River Joint Toll Bridge Commission (DRJTBC), New Jersey and Pennsylvania

As with the other three bi-state authorities, New Jersey Office of the State Comptroller officials reported that they have standing oversight of DRJTBC under New Jersey state law.[5] However, DRJTBC officials reported that the New Jersey Office of the State Comptroller does not have authority to audit or investigate DRJTBC because its audit authority is limited to entities within its state and does not extend to bi-state authorities. The New Jersey Office of the State Comptroller has not audited the DRJTBC, and it could not point to reciprocal legislation in Pennsylvania recognizing the New Jersey State Comptroller's audit authority. The Pennsylvania Department of the Auditor General reported that under Pennsylvania state law, the DRJTBC must submit biennially to a performance audit jointly conducted by the Auditor General of Pennsylvania and the State Auditor of New Jersey with a report to be issued every odd-numbered year. [6] The first report was to be completed by December 31, 1997. Similar legislation was passed in New Jersey that would require the Pennsylvania Auditor General and the New Jersey State Auditor to jointly conduct annual financial and management audits.[7] However, an official of Pennsylvania's Department of the Auditor General reported there is a conflict between the two states' laws with regard to the joint authority and audit schedule, and that this conflict needs to be resolved in order for the audit authority to be clear.[8] DRJTBC officials stated that neither state's laws amended DRJTBC's interstate compact because the laws were not identical and the two separate requirements for annual and biennial audits and different work products cannot be reconciled, and any amendments to the compact would require an act of Congress. As such, DRJTBC reported that neither New Jersey nor Pennsylvania state audit entities have authority to audit or investigate DRJTBC. The Pennsylvania Department of the Auditor General and the New Jersey State Auditor officials stated that none of the annual or biennial audits of DRJTBC cited in the state laws have been conducted

[5]N.J. Stat. § C52:15C.

[6]36 P.S. § 3401, Article IX.

[7]N.J. Stat. § 32:8-10, Article IX, which states that "the Auditor General of Pennsylvania and the State Auditor of New Jersey shall jointly conduct annual financial and management audits of expenditures and operations of the commission and shall submit a report of those audits to the Governors and Legislatures of the Commonwealth of Pennsylvania and the State of New Jersey."

[8]In February 2013, House Bill 620 was introduced in the Pennsylvania General Assembly that would amend this audit requirement.

by their offices either separately or jointly. During the course of our review, New Jersey State Auditor officials reported that its office sent the DRJTBC a letter to initiate an audit in July 2013, but DRJTBC rejected the request stating in a letter that the audit was not authorized by the DRJTBC interstate compact or by state laws in New Jersey and Pennsylvania. This disagreement between the DRJTBC and the State Auditor of New Jersey was yet to be resolved at the time of our report.

Delaware River Port Authority (DRPA), Pennsylvania and New Jersey	According to officials from Pennsylvania's Department of the Auditor General, it does not have the authority to audit or investigate DRPA because DRPA is an independent authority and not a state agency. A Pennsylvania Department of the Auditor General official also stated that because the Auditor General holds a standing, ex officio position as a voting member of the DRPA's Board of Commissioners, he or she cannot use his office to audit or investigate the DRPA, and has not conducted any audits of DRPA. According to New Jersey Office of the State Comptroller officials, the comptroller has standing oversight authority over DRPA, and exercised that authority in its 2012 investigative report. However, this investigation was conducted in response to the request of the governors of both states and with the approval of the DRPA board. Furthermore, New Jersey State Comptroller officials could not point to any reciprocal legislation in Pennsylvania recognizing standing authority to conduct future audits of DRPA. DRPA officials took no position as to whether New Jersey or Pennsylvania have standing audit authority and that any decision as to whether to adhere to any state audit requests would be a matter for its board to decide.
Port Authority of New York and New Jersey (PANYNJ), New York and New Jersey	Officials with the Office of the New York State Comptroller and the New Jersey Office of the State Comptroller officials stated that their offices have audit authority over the PANYNJ. The PANYNJ confirmed this audit authority; and while the Office of the New York State Comptroller has conducted several audits, the New Jersey Office of the State Comptroller has yet to do so. However, because the access authorities claimed by the New Jersey Office of the State Comptroller over PANYNJ in its enabling legislation[9] differ from the access authorities recognized by the

[9]N.J. Stat. § C52:15C would provide the New Jersey Comptroller with "complete access to all government records of public agencies."

PANYNJ,[10] it is unclear what specific authorities would be available to the New Jersey Office of the State Comptroller if it attempted to conduct an audit of PANYNJ. Furthermore, according to officials with the Office of the New York State Comptroller, the PANYNJ does not have the same requirements as New York state agencies to report its progress in implementing recommendations to the Office of the New York State Comptroller.

---

[10]The PANYNJ recognizes the New York and New Jersey Comptrollers' audit authority under state law in New York (McKinney's Unconsolidated Laws of New York, § 7071) and state law in New Jersey (New Jersey State Law 32:2-31, 32). The New York state statute states that "the comptroller of the state of New York and the comptroller of the state of New Jersey and their legally authorized representatives are hereby authorized and empowered from time to time to examine the accounts and books of the port of New York authority, including their receipts, disbursements, contracts, leases, sinking fund, investments and such other items referring to their financial standing and receipts and disbursements as such comptroller may deem proper. Such examination may be made by either comptroller at any time or by both comptrollers acting together."

Appendix V: GAO Contact and Staff Acknowledgments

Contact	Susan Fleming, (202) 512-2834 or flemings@gao.gov
Acknowledgments	In addition to the contact named above, Steve Cohen, Assistant Director; Matt Barranca; Melissa Bodeau; Mya Dinh; Dave Hooper; Joah Iannotta; Hannah Laufe; Josh Ormond; and Justin Reed made key contributions to this report.

GAO's Mission	The Government Accountability Office, the audit, evaluation, and investigative arm of Congress, exists to support Congress in meeting its constitutional responsibilities and to help improve the performance and accountability of the federal government for the American people. GAO examines the use of public funds; evaluates federal programs and policies; and provides analyses, recommendations, and other assistance to help Congress make informed oversight, policy, and funding decisions. GAO's commitment to good government is reflected in its core values of accountability, integrity, and reliability.
Obtaining Copies of GAO Reports and Testimony	The fastest and easiest way to obtain copies of GAO documents at no cost is through GAO's website (http://www.gao.gov). Each weekday afternoon, GAO posts on its website newly released reports, testimony, and correspondence. To have GAO e-mail you a list of newly posted products, go to http://www.gao.gov and select "E-mail Updates."
Order by Phone	The price of each GAO publication reflects GAO's actual cost of production and distribution and depends on the number of pages in the publication and whether the publication is printed in color or black and white. Pricing and ordering information is posted on GAO's website, http://www.gao.gov/ordering.htm.
	Place orders by calling (202) 512-6000, toll free (866) 801-7077, or TDD (202) 512-2537.
	Orders may be paid for using American Express, Discover Card, MasterCard, Visa, check, or money order. Call for additional information.
Connect with GAO	Connect with GAO on Facebook, Flickr, Twitter, and YouTube. Subscribe to our RSS Feeds or E-mail Updates. Listen to our Podcasts. Visit GAO on the web at www.gao.gov.
To Report Fraud, Waste, and Abuse in Federal Programs	Contact: Website: http://www.gao.gov/fraudnet/fraudnet.htm E-mail: fraudnet@gao.gov Automated answering system: (800) 424-5454 or (202) 512-7470
Congressional Relations	Katherine Siggerud, Managing Director, siggerudk@gao.gov, (202) 512-4400, U.S. Government Accountability Office, 441 G Street NW, Room 7125, Washington, DC 20548
Public Affairs	Chuck Young, Managing Director, youngc1@gao.gov, (202) 512-4800 U.S. Government Accountability Office, 441 G Street NW, Room 7149 Washington, DC 20548

Please Print on Recycled Paper.